Fire Over the Rock

Fire Over the Rock

The Great Siege of Gibraltar, 1779–1783

James Falkner

Pen & Sword
MILITARY

First published in Great Britain in 2009 by
PEN & SWORD MILITARY
an imprint of
Pen & Sword Books Ltd
47 Church Street
Barnsley
South Yorkshire
S70 2AS

ISBN 978 1 84415 915 4

Printed and bound in the UK by MPG Books

Pen & Sword Books Ltd incorporates the imprints of
Pen & Sword Aviation, Pen & Sword Family History, Pen & Sword Maritime,
Pen & Sword Military, Wharncliffe Local History, Pen & Sword Select,
Pen & Sword Military Classics, Leo Cooper, Remember When,
Seaforth Publishing and Frontline Publishing.

For a complete list of Pen & Sword titles please contact
PEN & SWORD BOOKS LIMITED
47 Church Street, Barnsley, South Yorkshire, S70 2AS, England
E-mail: enquiries@pen-and-sword.co.uk
Website: www.pen-and-sword.co.uk

Contents

List of Illustrations

List of Maps

Chronology of the Great Siege of Gibraltar

1775
April   Outbreak of the War of American Independence

1777
25 May   General Sir George Augustus Eliott takes up post as Governor of Gibraltar
6 December   France recognizes the United States of America

1778
17 June   Outbreak of hostilities between Great Britain and France

1779
12 April   Convention of Aranjuez; secret alliance between France and Spain
16 June   Spain declares war on Great Britain
21 June   Gibraltar blockaded by Spanish land and naval forces
5 July   Eliott first engages Don Antonio Barcelo's blockading squadron
12 September   British bombardment begins of the incomplete Spanish lines

1780
16–17 January   Admiral Sir George Rodney defeats Admiral de Langara's Spanish squadron off Cape St Vincent. Resupplies Gibraltar in the first relief of the garrison
6–7 June   Spanish fire ships' attack on Gibraltar harbour

1781
12 April   Second relief of Gibraltar by Vice Admiral George Darby

| | Spanish bombardment of Gibraltar town begins |
| 27 November | Grand Sortie by Gibraltar garrison to destroy Spanish forward batteries |

1782

15 February	Minorca captured by French forces under the Duc de Crillon
22 May	Sergeant Major Ince begins the tunnels
13–14 September	Spanish attack on Gibraltar with battering ships
17 October	Third relief of Gibraltar by Admiral Sir Richard Howe
20 October	Inconclusive naval battle off Cape Spartel

1783

20 January	Peace preliminaries signed in Paris
5 February	Blockade of Gibraltar lifted
10 March	News of peace terms reach Gibraltar
23 April	Victory review in Gibraltar
	Eliott made 1st Baron Heathfield of Gibraltar

Introduction

Noble Impartiality and Impatient Ambition

Nothing but 'Noble Impartiality' drove Spain to try to recover Gibraltar. At least, that was the rather spurious claim made at a time when Great Britain was striving to suppress rebellion in North America. By the summer of 1779, British forces had been engaged for four years in what seemed to be the fruitless task of trying to remain in possession of the American colonies. Considerable attention also had to be devoted to securing important territories in the West Indies, and maintaining influence across the Indian Ocean. Without much doubt, had Great Britain not been so deeply engaged in the task of trying to fight a war in North America, Spain would not have tried to regain Gibraltar in such a fashion. This was particularly so as London had indicated, on several occasions, that the Rock was not really worth holding, and some subtle diplomacy by Madrid might have achieved a great deal of good.

It was not altogether surprising that Spain took advantage of this powerful strategic distraction first to blockade, and then attack, the British garrison on the Rock. The moment must have seemed to King Carlos III and his ministers in Madrid to be very ripe, with British naval and military forces so heavily engaged elsewhere.[1] This was a significant misjudgement. Although few Britons wished to lose the American possessions, troublesome as they were, few also who were well enough informed to come to a judgement thought that the colonies could be held against their will, or that it was worth the enormous effort and expense to do so. Significant numbers of Loyalists were fighting alongside the British to suppress the rebellion, but French support, which could not be properly countered at the time, would prove crucial to the success of the rebels. This was particularly so as so much effort had, because of Spanish opportunism, to be devoted to operations to hold on to Gibraltar and Port Mahon on the island of Minorca, the valuable bases for the Royal Navy in the western Mediterranean.

The rapidly growing British Empire, still in comparative infancy in the 1770s, depended upon trade on the high seas, and security and ease of navigation through the Mediterranean was a key factor in this strategic endeavour. British trade interests in the spice and sugar islands of the Caribbean, across the Indian sub-continent, and in the Mediterranean, were of greater potential value and importance to Great Britain than holding on to rebellious and very unprofitable colonies in North America. No imperial power relished the loss of territory, but the cost could be just too high, especially when that task was fast proving to be fruitless, thanks to French mischief-making. On the other hand, territory that had a tangible and recognizable benefit, such as a naval base in a strategically important location like Gibraltar, a base which actually had the capability to be held, would merit the attention, cost and effort necessary for a prolonged and successful defence – a military epic in the making.

The Spanish naval and military commanders found that the British would fight hard to hold on to Gibraltar. This was a campaign that would catch the imagination and admiration of George III's subjects, ministers and military commanders alike, in a way that the distant war in North America would not, even if the King seemed less than enthusiastic at times about retaining possession of the Rock. This should have come as no real surprise, for British interest in securing and holding the place as a base for the Royal Navy had a lengthy, if somewhat ambivalent, history, it first having been considered as long ago as October 1625. 'The Bay of Gibraltar is a very safe and commodious one; a fine port for the trading ships coming from the Mediterranean.'[2] Thirty years later, the Lord Protector of the Commonwealth, Oliver Cromwell, had Samuel Pepys, Secretary of the Navy at the time, draw up a plan to undermine the loyalty of the Spanish Governor. 'With six nimble frigates lodged there to do the Spaniards more harm.'[3] All this came to nothing, but Gibraltar had from time to time been used by the squadrons of the 'Maritime Powers' (England and Holland) throughout the late seventeenth century, as an entry-port into the western Mediterranean, the trade route along which the valuable Smyrna convoys made their way towards the English Channel, laden with their exotic luxuries from the Ottoman Empire and the East. Even so, the apparently idiosyncratic determination by Great Britain to keep possession of Gibraltar, at whatever cost was required, was not foreseen by the Spanish King and his ministers in 1779.

Leaving to one side the almost unavoidable problems of alliance warfare, with Spanish and French commanders striving manfully, but not always with success, to work together to good effect, the simple fact was that the British defence of Gibraltar was an operation that could succeed, in a way that the more complex efforts to defend Britain's other outpost in the Mediterranean, the island of Minorca, would not. By nature a formidable fortress, if the Rock could not be taken by outright assault – and its defences had been greatly improved in the years leading up to the events of 1779 – then the garrison might still be blockaded and starved out. There was little chance to grow vegetables, and fresh water was always a concern, having to be gathered from rainfall; every ounce of powder and shot, every stick of firewood, piece of biscuit and scrap of meat, and each strip of linen or shoe-leather, would have to be forced through any blockade, in the teeth of tough resistance. The Royal Navy was found to have the capability to do this, not once (a significant achievement on its own), but in three notable operations, across the 1,100 inhospitable miles of stormy seas from the ports in southern England and Ireland. The Spanish Navy, for a variety of implausible reasons, proved incapable of preventing this resupply, either on the high seas or by imposing a tight enough close blockade, and their French allies were no more successful.

There was also the distinct character and robust no-nonsense nature of the commander of the besieged garrison in Gibraltar – 62-year-old General Sir George Augustus Eliott (subsequently made 1st Baron Heathfield of Gibraltar, and an acknowledged British Hero). A highly capable soldier, well-educated, rather austere, and an ardent student of military technique and thought, Eliott's early training as an engineer officer (while holding a commission as an officer of light cavalry), suited him very nicely to the arduous task he was given in command of the troops on the Rock. Zealous and resolute, although not without a dry sense of humour, teetotal and a vegetarian, a man not to be daunted or to lightly relinquish any task entrusted to his care, Eliott was, arguably, just the person for the demanding operations to come. (See Appendix 1.)

The last real attempt to regain Gibraltar by force of arms, which led to the longest formal siege in history, was not doomed from the very start. The forces that Spain, and to a lesser degree, France, devoted to the effort were considerable, both on land and at sea, and their troops and seamen were commanded by accomplished officers of fine reputation. At the instruction of Carlos III, the Spanish Army had been reformed and re-equipped upon modern lines in recent years. Officers' military education had improved, particularly in siege methods, the Corps of Royal Engineers had long had a fine reputation, and the artillery adopted the French Gribeauval standard calibre system. Travellers in Spain at this time commented on the good discipline and level of training of the soldiers they saw. The Armada Espagnol was numerous and powerful, going through a period of great expansion and shipbuilding in the royal shipyards of Ferrol and Havana, with many vessels being of a noticeably better design than those in service with the Royal Navy (the French ships enjoyed this same design advantage). The Spanish naval commanders had learned their hard trade during the long campaigns waged against the corsairs who operated along the Barbary coast of North Africa, where, it was said, there was piracy without and anarchy within. They sustained and maintained the huge worldwide empire, and acquired a distinguished record of adventurous exploration, although the training of their ships' crews left something to be desired at times.

At the time of the Great Siege, the Royal Navy was badly overcommitted, with operations in the North Atlantic, along the American seaboard and in the Indian Ocean, providing defence for the English Channel, and contending with prickly and unpredictable Armed Neutrality in the North Sea and the Baltic. Overstretch was very evident, yet the garrisons in Gibraltar and Minorca had also to be sustained and the omens for a Spanish success must have seemed to those in Madrid to be very promising.

The Spanish and French besiegers of Gibraltar showed ingenuity, persistence and undeniable bravery in their efforts, but they would fail absolutely to overcome Eliott and his indomitable garrison. Although the end result of the campaign can be seen clearly with the benefit of hindsight, that outcome was by no means certain as the siege and blockade lasted. The weeks of bombardment went wearily on, casualty lists lengthened, and the troops in the garrison tightened their belts, and ticked off the long passing days on their fingers. All became more anxious and more hungry, while their wives and children crouched in squalid camps, wincing under the Spanish fire and suffering the fearful ravages of smallpox and scurvy. Officers grew older and duller, fretting at their missed chances for glory during what seemed, at the time, to be an arid and forgotten campaign. Two years into the siege, those officers would petition the Governor with their concerns, asking him to ensure that their prospects for promotion did not suffer as a result of being confined in Gibraltar for so long. Of course, to have been at the Great Siege would, in time, be regarded as a mark of real merit and honour, something to tell children and grandchildren about, and no disadvantage to preferment at all, but that was all in the future and could not be imagined or foreseen.

An efficient and close blockade of any garrison, to deny everything necessary to sustain life, in a campaign not overly time-dependent upon the fine-weather months of summer, must always succeed. Despite this, Spain, although having the natural advantages of numerous good ports close at hand from which her fleet could operate, never devoted sufficient naval strength to the vital task of the close blockade of the Rock to make it really effective; nor were the efforts of the Spanish and French fleets co-ordinated well enough to make their superior numbers count on the high seas, where the cruising squadrons of the Royal Navy had to be confronted and beaten, if the garrison was to be starved out. This was an unavoidable fact – Gibraltar could not be held if the Royal Navy failed to supply the inhabitants, civil and military alike.

The Spanish sea-captains and their crews were kept short of supplies, their men sometimes went unpaid, and the antiquated command structure in the Armada Espagnol, whereby the fleet commanders were excluded from the actual handling of the ships, made for operations that were noticeably lacking in bite. Carlos III was prone to issuing instructions to his admirals which, although undoubtedly meant to be helpful, when received were often irrelevant to the situation at the time – delay and confusion resulted. The Spanish naval commanders might be suspected of having insufficient imagination to see that they should take prudent risks to achieve success, but had too much imagination when foreseeing that defeat might attend their efforts. This was doubly so after Admiral Sir George Rodney destroyed two Spanish squadrons in short order, early in 1780, while on his way with a major convoy to relieve the garrison on the Rock for the first time. The spirit in Spain's naval effort in the campaign to regain Gibraltar never really recovered. By comparison, the Royal Navy, although over-committed and undermanned, has rarely shown itself to better advantage than in its continuous operations to sustain Eliott and his men between 1779 and 1783.

The longstanding sense of grievance among the Spanish over the whole matter stemmed from the belief that Gibraltar had been taken away under false pretences in 1704 during the War of the Spanish Succession. Ostensibly this had been on behalf of Archduke Charles of Austria, at a moment when England and Spain were not even at war. The Rock was then permanently wrested away in an unduly punitive peace settlement in 1713, under treaty terms that Great Britain (as it became from 1707 onwards) promptly and repeatedly broke. This treaty, it could be argued, had not truly reflected the situation 'on the ground' at the time, as Great Britain and her allies had failed to win the war in Spain. Clearly, what could or could not be achieved on the ground was not always reflected in what could be had by skilful negotiation, in comfortable salons far away from the field of battle. All this fuelled the Spanish desire to secure the return of the Rock, an aim not necessarily unreasonable or illogical. On several occasions during the eighteenth century, and with varying degrees of sincerity, the British discussed with Spain the handing back of sovereignty over the place, if other concessions, most notably the continuation of the occupation of Minorca with its valuable deep-water port of Mahon, could be guaranteed in exchange. Occasional reports of doubts in London over whether Gibraltar was worth the expense of maintaining in a state of defence during peacetime, or worth going to war for, would encourage Carlos III and his advisers in Madrid, and the tentative negotiations would stutter on even throughout the years of the Great Siege.

In 1779 it seemed to many that the determination to hold on to Gibraltar at all costs in the face of a vigorous Spanish military campaign was probably lacking. Surely then, when British attention was fixed on the colonies in North America, this might be the right time to strike. Fine feelings are all very well, and it certainly seemed to cast Spain in a poor light that it cynically chose to take advantage of London's difficulties in this way, but in time of war it often pays to seize those opportunities that are offered. King George III had once remarked that the continued British hold on the Rock would ensure 'a constant lurking enmity between England and Spain' – undoubtedly this was so, and what was seen in Madrid as a historic and irrational injustice could perhaps now be put right.[4]

If possession of Gibraltar had no tangible strategic value for Great Britain, the effort and expense of resisting the Spanish attack would be counted a folly. This was particularly so as the necessary diversion of resources to hold the Rock put British military and naval efforts in North America under real strain at a perilous time. 'We ought not to lose sight of its distance from home,' wrote Major Hugh Debbing, an engineer officer who surveyed the Rock and reported back to London on its capability to be defended against a determined aggressor, 'separated from us by the continent of Europe, that our fleet may at some critical time have more necessary and indispensable employment.'[5] The comment was perceptive; the ability of the Royal Navy to operate in the Mediterranean, and the protection to merchant shipping that this ensured, was acknowledged as being of great importance. Whatever the cost, the retention of Gibraltar, and also Port Mahon in Minorca if that could be achieved, was undoubtedly seen as a legitimate use of otherwise scarce resources.

Any formal siege of a fortified place only becomes such when the besieging forces so closely invest or blockade the garrison that no support or replenishment is possible without extraordinary efforts. Allowing for the fact that Gibraltar was bounded, on all but a very narrow land frontage on the northern side, by the sea, the importance of naval power was obvious where any attempt to overcome the defences of the Rock was concerned. Given the proven capabilities of the Royal Navy, upon which the resupply of the garrison depended, and what became evident as the inability of the Spanish and French navies to prevent these vital operations for long, it might be thought that in fact, no 'siege' of Gibraltar was ever established, in a formal sense. John Muller wrote in a learned treatise on siege warfare intended for the education of young officers:

> To block up [blockade] a place is to surround it with a sufficient number of troops, as to prevent any succour or provision being thrown into it. *The intent is to reduce a garrison by famine* [my italics]. A place should never be blockaded, but on a certainty that there is a small quantity of provisions in it, otherwise it would require too much time, and, perhaps, not be taken at last.[6]

He might almost have been writing about Gibraltar. There were certainly a finite amount of provisions on the Rock at any one time, but the magazines and storehouses would be replenished at lengthy but regular intervals by merchant ships convoyed in under the protection of the

Royal Navy. Given all this, it can be argued that the Spanish forces on land and at sea never successfully established either a real siege or a complete blockade, despite the valour of their sea-captains, and great reliance appears instead to have rested on hopes of a failure in the will of the British, both at home and in Gibraltar, to hold the Rock when all eyes in London were thought to be firmly fixed on retaining the American colonies, and little else.

Of course, after proving unable to hold those same American colonies, there was a corresponding greater British determination, perhaps even a bitter and perverse determination, not to be driven out of the western Mediterranean. Gibraltar became a touchstone by which the ability of Great Britain to endure, despite disproportionately heavy odds, and come through with success was measured. In addition, and as a rather more practical consideration, it was felt that the valuable deep-water anchorage at Port Mahon could only be held if the Royal Navy also had Gibraltar as a secure base, guaranteeing relatively easy passage through the Straits. On the other hand, if Minorca could not be held, and France had once before removed a British garrison by force, in the 1750s, then this would have relatively little effect on the ability of the British to retain a garrison on the Rock as an entry port to the Mediterranean Sea. Gibraltar, therefore, was valuable if Minorca could be held, and even more so if that island was lost.

The defence of Gibraltar by the British and Hanoverian garrison under George Augustus Eliott was an undeniably epic operation; at three years, seven months and twelve days it was almost certainly the longest continuous formal siege in all recorded history. The place could not be overwhelmed simply by a storm across the flat and barren isthmus that linked the Rock to the mainland; the defences were too formidable for that, and there was no way to outflank them, other than to approach in boats across the Bay, exposed to the shot and shell of the powerful batteries on the westward side. It was to the credit of the Spanish and French commanders of the various stages of the siege, that, despite the general expectation in Madrid and Paris that Gibraltar would be taken, and frequent exhortations sent to them to that effect, they did not often stoop to waste the lives of their soldiers in futile attacks which held little prospect of success. On the other hand, those same military officers may certainly be criticized for the initial lack of urgency in establishing effective battery positions with which to threaten the Rock, and a failure to fully co-ordinate their efforts with their naval colleagues.

A heavy artillery bombardment, against a garrison weakened by privation, dull routine and disease, in conjunction with infantry assaults and, more promisingly perhaps, by simultaneous amphibious landings on the western side and southern extremity of Gibraltar, would have held out an intriguing possibility of success. What Admiral Rooke and the Prince of Hesse-Darmstadt had achieved in 1704 when Spain lost the Rock could surely be repeated if the preparations were sufficiently thorough. Still, if an assault on the place was not practical – and how it could be attempted was no simple matter – the garrison, encumbered with the civilian population and service families, crammed together in poor conditions with scarce supplies of provisions and fresh water, could surely be starved out. In the event, the inability of the Spanish and French commanders to establish and maintain an effective naval blockade proved decisive: 'No power whatever can take the place, unless a plague, pestilence, famine or the want of ordnance, musketry, and ammunition, or some unforeseen stroke of Providence should happen.'[7] Despite the sustained attempts of the besiegers, there was no such unforeseen stroke to seriously imperil the garrison, and the Rock would be firmly held for Great Britain.

One unfortunate young Spanish officer wrote in his report, shortly before his battery position was overrun one night and he received a mortal wound, that 'Nothing extraordinary had happened.' Much the same could be said for periods of the Great Siege, when the opposing forces seemed at times inclined to stare each other out – the besiegers expecting hunger to achieve victory for them, while the besieged scanned the horizon in hopes that the topsails of a Royal Navy escorted resupply convoy were approaching. To attempt to list the routine daily activities of the garrison on the one hand, or of the besieging troops on the other, would very soon become repetitious and, to quote a veteran of the siege, 'tedious'. So, I have attempted to tell the remarkable story of the Great Siege of the Rock by concentrating on the principal events both on land and at sea, interspersing the narrative with those anecdotes which seem most to give the flavour of what the troops and seamen on both sides, and the women and children on the Rock, had to endure.

1

A Little World of Itself

'Gibraltar is situated in Andalusia, the most southern province of Spain ... a little world of itself,' wrote John Drinkwater, a veteran of the years of the Great Siege.[1] Known to the Berbers as Gabal Al Tariq (Tariq's Mount), the rocky promontory, or Bill, rises dramatically almost sheer out of the waters of the western Mediterranean Sea. A mere three miles long north to south, half a mile across, and 1,403 feet at its highest point, it is connected to the Spanish mainland by a low, sandy, isthmus about 2,000 yards in length. From Europa Point, the southernmost part of the Rock, the port of Ceuta on the North African shore is only about fifteen miles away across the Straits of Gibraltar, which form the valuable strategic gateway from the Atlantic Ocean to the Mediterranean.

> The Bay of Gibraltar is a very safe and commodious one; a fine port for the trading ships coming from the Mediterranean; they can bear to windward as far as this bay, but no further. This impediment arises from the current running so forcefully in these narrow straits.[2]

The Rock was captured from Spain on 24 July 1704 by an amphibious English and Dutch force under the command of Admiral Sir George Rooke and Prince George of Hesse-Darmstadt, during the early part of the long War of the Spanish Succession. The complex dynastic dispute that plagued Europe at the time had erupted into open conflict two years earlier, when a Grand Alliance formed by England, Holland and Austria sought to limit the expanding power of King Louis XIV's France. The principal aim of the Alliance, however, was to ensure that the huge Spanish empire of Spain should be divided, on an equitable basis, between two rival claimants to the throne in Madrid – vacated in November 1700 at the death of the childless King Carlos II – Philip of Anjou of France, youngest son of the French King, and Archduke Charles of Austria, second son of the Habsburg Emperor, Leopold I.

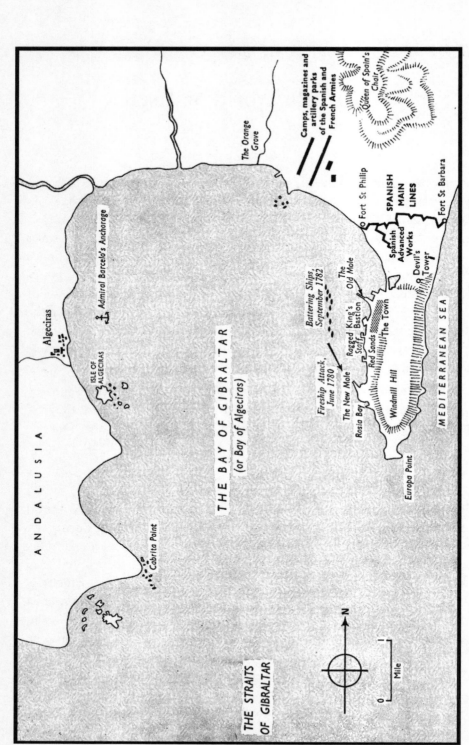

The Bay of Gibraltar.

No one really wanted war, not least because of the cost involved, but equally no one had seemed capable of avoiding it, once Carlos II died leaving the throne in his will to the Duc d'Anjou. As it was, by 1704 the young Frenchman, Philip (Felipe) V, was comfortably installed in Madrid, and was gaining the acceptance of much of the Spanish people as their monarch. The forces of the Grand Alliance pursued an expensive and fruitless campaign in Portugal (which became a partner in that alliance), Aragon and Catalonia, in an effort to have the Austrian Archduke (Charles/Carlos III) installed in his place. So it was that Rooke and his seventy-strong Anglo-Dutch fleet were cruising off the Rock of Gibraltar in the summer of 1704, having failed to make either a successful landing of troops in Valencia, or to bring the French Mediterranean Fleet to battle. Rooke and Hesse-Darmstadt had considered making an assault on Cadiz, but instead decided to launch a surprise attack on the Rock, where the garrison was rumoured to be both small and ill-prepared. A summons to the Spanish Governor, Don Diego de Salinas, to submit and declare his allegiance to the Archduke was firmly rejected. The Governor had recently protested to Madrid, in vain, at the inadequacy of his small garrison and the poor state of the defences; it was too late for, after a short bombardment on 21 July, nearly two thousand Dutch and English troops and marines were landed by boat on the isthmus – 'a plain of white sand' – between the Rock and the mainland. Two days later a party of marines and seamen under the command of a Captain Whitaker landed on the New Mole on the western side of the Rock, covered by the fire of sixteen English and six Dutch warships.

The landing party met what appeared to be only light resistance at first, but then the Spanish soldiers blew a well-placed defensive mine that killed and wounded several dozen of the attackers. De Salinas, in fact, put up a creditable defence, as his duty to King Philip V required. According to some reports, only about eighty of his troops were fully trained, and the Duc de Nouailles wrote that they were 'without armaments, and without cannon in proper working order'.[3] This seems to be an exaggeration, and the defenders were plainly spirited in their endeavours, as the very successful blowing of the deadly mine at the New Mole demonstrated. The attacking force suffered no fewer than 320 killed and wounded before Gibraltar was won for Carlos III and the Grand Alliance.

De Salinas had little choice but to capitulate, on 24 July, and his valour was rewarded with Rooke according him and his surviving soldiers the honours of war; they marched out of Gibraltar and made their way over the isthmus to Spain. Plainly, this was not meant to be a permanent abandonment of territory, but the submission by the Spanish commander of a fortified place in the face of overwhelming odds, a clear, but very localized, military defeat. The unpalatable alternative for the Governor was to fight on and to waste the lives of his soldiers needlessly, but as so often, possession may be seen as being nine points of the law. If Spain wanted the territory back, some neat diplomatic footwork was required, or a resoundingly successful feat of arms.

Unfortunately, discipline deteriorated very quickly, and the wretched civilian residents of the Rock had to endure a sack of the place by the victorious soldiers and marines, who broke open the wine-shops and were soon, in many cases, roaring drunk. 'Outrages', in the restrained language of the time, were committed, but, both violent and fuddled, singly or in groups, the Allied soldiers and marines soon found that the narrow streets and alleys of the Old Town were dangerous places in which to loiter; a Spanish commentator wrote, 'Many females suffered insults and outrages, whence arose numerous sanguinary acts of vengeance on the part of the inhabitants, who murdered the perpetrators and threw their bodies into wells and sewers.'[4] Calm was eventually restored by the simple expedient of hanging some of the perpetrators of the outrages (on both sides), and letting the bodies swing from makeshift gibbets at the side of the alleys. In the tragic circumstances, it was almost inevitable that most of the unfortunate populace would choose to leave Gibraltar as soon as they could. The refugees mostly settled in the small town of San Roques on the mainland, at the foot of the hill known as the Queen of Spain's Chair, and in clear sight of their old homes on the Rock. The British and Dutch were left in possession of a ruined and deserted town and fortress, and more interestingly, a most useful harbour. Once there, it seemed to make good strategic sense to hold on to the place for the time being.

As soon as Gibraltar was secured, Admiral Rooke took his ships off to Tetuan on the North African coast to take on board fresh water. On 13 August 1704 (Old System, eleven days behind the New System in use on the Continent), he fought a major but inconclusive naval engagement off Malaga, against a French fleet under the Comte de Toulouse, who had been reinforced with Spanish vessels and could deploy fifty ships-of-the-line to Rooke's forty-one. The sprawling battle lasted all day, and saw considerable expenditure in powder and shot (which Rooke could ill afford after his bombardment of the Rock, having had no opportunity to replenish his magazines), but neither side lost a vessel. 'The Count of Toulouse met the fleet under Admiral Rooke off Malaga,' the Duc de St Simon wrote, 'and fought with it from ten in the morning till eight at night ... It was long since such a tenacious and furious contact had been seen at sea.'[5] The French and Spanish ships eventually drew off, even though they had the weather gauge, and so did the British and Dutch, neither side being in a fit state to pursue the other very far. Rooke's casualties were 2,758 killed and wounded, very similar to those of Toulouse's squadron, whose loss was estimated at nearly 3,000.

Rooke brought his battered ships into the shelter of Gibraltar (Algeciras) Bay in the lee of the Rock, to repair and refit for eight days; Sir Cloudesley Shovell remembered that there was hardly a vessel that did not have to replace one mast, and some had to replace them all. When powder and shot had been redistributed around the fleet, there were scarcely ten rounds a gun, not nearly enough to sustain another general action, and after landing detachments of seamen to reinforce the garrison, he set out for England. This was the first of many such occasions when the Royal Navy would make use of the Rock in this way, under the protection of the guns of a British garrison.

Once it was learned that Gibraltar had been occupied by the Allies, Philip V moved whatever troops could be spared from other fronts southwards as fast as they could manage, to attempt its recovery. A Spanish and French army of over 12,000 troops, under the command of the Marquis de Villadarias, was soon within sight of the Rock, where the garrison had been reinforced with units drawn from the languishing Allied expedition to Portugal. On 15 October, a heavy bombardment of the rather dilapidated defences was begun, and two weeks later the first of several spirited attempts to surprise the fortress at night was made, but this attempt was driven off by the grenadier companies of the 3,000-strong garrison after some smart work with the bayonet. The French Marshal Tessé was sent to take command of operations, and a powerful blockading squadron under Admiral Pontis arrived off the Rock. Tessé was not impressed by the arrangements for the siege that he found, or the poor state of the squalid camp and the half-empty storehouses and magazines. The Spanish commander, Villadarias, for his part, was offended to have a French officer appointed over him, and he resigned his commission – tellingly, the letter he sent went to King Louis XIV in Versailles, not to his grandson in Madrid.

The blockade and siege continued with little success and varying energy through the winter months, some 78,000 artillery rounds being fired at the garrison, with little effect other than to mangle and maim, and keep the weary defenders on the alert to repulse any assault that was made:

> The enemy attacked us this day, at break of day, at the Round tower and the breach above it. They began this attack with 500 [French] grenadiers sustained by 1,000 Spaniards ... They threaten us heavily with a general assault which has kept us night and day under arms. Our daily loss is 20, 30 and sometimes 40 men a day wounded or killed.[6]

On 10 March 1705, the Royal Navy squadron operating out of Lisbon under the command of Sir John Leake sank or drove off five of the blockading French ships, and resupplied the garrison, which had diminished through casualties and sickness to an effective strength of only 1,300 all ranks, too few to hold the place against a moderately determined assault. Events were moving fast elsewhere in Spain, particularly in Catalonia, where the Allies were gaining ground, and Tessé and his troops could no longer be spared for the siege – at best, always a side-show to the wider war. So, soon afterwards the French and Spaniards withdrew from their forward positions, and then most of them marched away, and Gibraltar was left securely to the British. Unfortunately, Prince George of Hesse-Darmstadt, perhaps the best field commander the Allies had in Spain, was killed shortly afterwards at the capture of Barcelona, to the detriment of their campaign from then onwards; meanwhile, a rather half-hearted and intermittent blockade of the Rock was maintained by the Spanish until the end of the war.

Gibraltar had been captured in the name of the Austrian claimant to the throne in Madrid, Archduke Charles (Carlos) III, and Hesse-Darmstadt acknowledged this in the terms of capitulation offered to De Salinas.[7] However, it suited the Royal Navy in particular to have the valuable harbour safely in British hands, for the convenient use of their increasingly active cruising squadrons in the Mediterranean. Charles III appointed General Ramos as his Governor, but he soon resigned the post, and a British officer, Roger Eliott, took his place. Despite the involvement of Dutch ships and troops in the seizure of Gibraltar, it was soon made quite clear to the States-General of Holland and to the Imperial Court in Vienna that this was to be regarded as a British matter in which their allies had no real lasting interest. The value of the Rock in sustaining the expanding activities of the Royal Navy in the Mediterranean was plain, and despite some quite natural resentment among the other parties to the Grand Alliance at such a dismissive attitude, Queen Anne and her ministers were adamant, and got their way. So, at the Treaty of Utrecht which brought the War of the Spanish Succession to an end in 1713, possession of Gibraltar was ceded by Spain in perpetuity to Great Britain, as was the island of Minorca, which had been seized by troops under the command of Earl James Stanhope in 1708; Clause X of the treaty read in contradictory part:

> His Catholic Majesty [Philip V] yields absolutely to Great Britain all claims to the full and entire propriety [in full right] of the Town and Castle of Gibraltar [le pleine et entière propriété de la Ville et du Château], together with the Port, fortifications and forts belonging thereto; And he gives of the said propriety to be held and enjoyed absolutely with all manner of right for ever ...
> The above named propriety to be yielded to Great Britain without any territorial jurisdiction [sans aucune Jurisdiction Territoriale] ... Her Britannic Majesty, at the request of the Catholic King, does consent and agree, that no leave shall be given, under any pretence whatever, for Jews or Moors, to reside and have their dwellings in the said town of Gibraltar.[8]

The Spanish plenipotentiaries at the negotiations had not been consulted over this clause until after it had been agreed by the French representatives – they were presented with a *fait accompli*. The place had been captured in the name of a Spanish King (Charles III), but had then been appropriated by Great Britain for its own use and advantage.[9]

The status of Gibraltar, on the face of things, has remained unchanged, if a little ambiguous, ever since. This is so despite efforts by Great Britain to exchange the Rock for seemingly more valuable outposts in the Mediterranean and the West Indies, or to gain advantageous trading terms with Spain and its huge empire. In 1717, the Secretary of State,

James Stanhope, urged his Cabinet colleagues that the Rock should be given up to Madrid, as not worth the trouble and expense of maintaining the garrison. He was overruled the following year, but his was not a lone voice on the matter. Certainly, the £90,000 it cost annually to maintain the garrison even in peacetime was regretted, and in 1721, King George I wrote to Philip V offering 'to make use of the first favourable opportunity to regulate this Article (touching the restitution of Gibraltar) with the Consent of my Parliament'.[10] No such consent was forthcoming, of course, so nothing came of the offer, and the Spanish monarch perceptively commented that the note was 'so darkly worded and that which His Majesty promised so faintly expressed that it really and strictly engaged for nothing'.

This had not meant that all was peace and quiet for long, once Marshal Tessé marched his troops away from the camp at San Roques in 1705, and gave up the first real attempt to get the place back for Spain. Fifteen years later, the small garrison of three under-strength and poorly equipped infantry battalions on the Rock, commanded by Major Hetherington, had to be quickly reinforced with 500 troops from Minorca. A Spanish squadron under the Marquis de Leda had begun to assemble in Gibraltar Bay, but eventually the ships sailed off to reinforce the Spanish enclave of Ceuta on the North African coast, the Marquis having realized that, once reinforced, the Rock was too firmly held for anything much to be attempted. In 1726 a fresh concentration of Spanish troops between Algeciras and San Roques caused concern, and the following January a large force under the Count de los Torres, Viceroy of Navarre, advanced upon the isthmus. He knew very well that without a strong naval squadron to control the Bay and its approaches, whatever might be attempted was unlikely to succeed, but with about 18,000 troops under his command, the renewed Spanish activity had to be treated with due attention by the garrison on the Rock.

The Governor of Gibraltar, Lord Portmore, sent a request to the Viceroy that he should pull his troops back, warning that otherwise they would be fired on by the guns of the garrison. This message was haughtily rejected; the implication was that the British enjoyed control only over the land they actually stood on, and that de los Torres would march his troops wherever he wished on Spanish soil. He was 'on his master's ground, and was not answerable to any other person for his conduct'.[11] As there was no state of war between Britain and Spain at the time, Portmore could do little more than quickly send for reinforcements. He had also flooded a roughly triangular area of marshy land in front of the Old Moorish Castle on the North Face of the Rock, which became known as the Inundation, 'about 200 yards in length, and 60 in breadth. It is always kept filled with water, nearly man-height, from sluices to let in the sea from the bay'.[12] A near-permanent and very useful obstacle to augment the forward defences was thereby created, narrowing the approaches to the Old Town. This was in addition to Willis's Battery, which was placed high above the Moorish Castle, with commanding fields of fire across the low-lying ground of the isthmus.

During February 1727 Spanish engineers began to erect strong batteries on the Neutral Ground. This was plainly a highly provocative act, and the guns of the garrison (once again reinforced from the British troops in Minorca) began firing on the workmen labouring on the battery positions, on 11 February. The ordnance was, however, old and in many cases defective; the powder supply was damp, so that the fire was not very effective, although some 25,000 rounds would be expended. The number of times the guns burst while in action caused more concern to the gunners, and more injuries, than to their intended targets the Spanish labourers; of the 126 artillery pieces in action, no fewer than seventy-eight burst while firing. The garrison was supported by a Royal Navy squadron of fourteen warships operating in the Bay under Rear Admiral Charles Wager, and their broadsides hampered Spanish attempts at sapping and mining their way towards the defences on the Rock. Despite this, on 20 February, a brisk bombardment by ninety Spanish guns was opened on the defence from the newly established batteries.

Apart from some skirmishing by the outposts, and a small sortie by the garrison, not much more happened. The Royal Navy had no real difficulty in resupplying the garrison from Minorca, and the numbers of the troops gradually increased from fewer than 1,500 to 6,100, without much hindrance. The 1st English Foot Guards were among those troops shipped in. The siege, such as it was, became a rather futile affair, although one of the more agreeable aspects was the habit of the Spanish gunners of retiring after the lunch-time meal, to take their siesta in the heat of the day, enabling the garrison on the Rock to do very much the same. Tedium seems to have been the abiding memory, with one soldier writing, 'Here is nothing to do nor any news, all things being dormant and in suspense with the harmless (lawless) diversions of drinking, dancing, revelling, whoring, gambling and other innocent debaucheries to pass the time.'[13] One determined attempt was made by the Spanish sappers to undermine the Rock below Willis's Battery, but the hard substrata soon defeated their pickaxes and crowbars. The weather was bad, disease set in among the besieging troops, and their camp hospitals were soon crowded with the sick and the dying; desertions from the Spanish lines steadily grew in frequency.

Peace was declared once more between the two countries, and in June 1727 the Spanish troops began to withdraw and dismantle their battery positions. The Treaty of Seville, agreed in 1729, confirmed the re-establishment of friendly relations between Spain and Great Britain and also, coincidentally, the relevant portions of the 1713 Treaty of Utrecht, although there was no explicit reference to Gibraltar, and just where sovereignty of the place exactly lay. Lord Townsend commented to one of the British negotiators at the talks in Breda on a fresh Spanish suggestion that they should regain sovereignty in exchange for favourable trading concessions:

> What you propose in relation to Gibraltar is certainly very reasonable, and is exactly conformable to the opinion which you know I have always entertained concerning that place [but] I am afraid that the bare mention of a proposal which carried the most distant appearance of laying England under an obligation of ever parting with the place would be sufficient to put the whole nation in a flame.[14]

This attitude seemed to settle things, the two countries tacitly agreed to put the question on the shelf, and the Rock was quiet once again.

In 1730 the Marquis de Verboom, Chief Engineer of the Spanish Corps of Royal Engineers, was instructed to construct two large redoubts, named Fort St Barbara and Fort St Philip, at either end of the fortified line gradually taking shape across the neck of the isthmus, about 1,500 yards from the front of the North Face. These, not surprisingly, soon became known as the Spanish Lines, or La Línea de Contravalacíon, and they would play a major part in the Great Siege (the two forts were eventually blown up by the British in February 1810, to prevent their occupation by French forces). The guns mounted in Fort St Philip had the ability to cover the best anchorages at the time with fire, but, on the other hand, these new works also constituted the first formal barrier to be erected between the Rock and the Spanish mainland. Their construction might almost be construed as tacit acceptance of the status quo – that Gibraltar was British, for the foreseeable future at any rate, and there was not a lot that the Spanish could do about it, other than to better secure their border against any further British incursion.

Throughout much of the next fifty years, Gibraltar was left in peace, although Spain could not be reconciled to the British possession either of the Rock or Minorca, a concern that was certainly shared by France where the island was concerned. During the strangely named War of Jenkins' Ear in 1743, the British privateer, *Pulteney*, was intercepted in the Bay by two oar-driven Spanish xebecs, and had to fight her way clear. The dilapidated old Spanish Town, the population of which had shrunk to almost nothing when the civilians left in haste in 1704, once again expanded along the slopes overlooking the Bay. With a few exceptions, these new residents were not Spaniards, but mostly came from Genoa, Sardinia, North Africa and elsewhere. By 1777, nearly a third of the population was Jewish, quite contrary to the strict terms of the Treaty of Utrecht (and providing one of the Spanish arguments that as those terms had been deliberately and repeatedly broken by Great Britain, they were null and void).[15] Spain continued to look for the return of the fortress, and the government in London considered giving the Rock up, as being hardly worth the trouble and expense of its keeping – certainly, the prospect of gaining favourable trading concessions in Spain's empire in the Americas was attractive, compared to the arguable advantages of holding on to Gibraltar in the face of Spanish hostility. The guarantee of free passage through the Straits of Gibraltar was an undoubted asset, but, while the place remained in British hands, it was impossible to fully re-establish good diplomatic relations between Madrid and London. Unsurprisingly, the French hovered in the wings, eager to make mischief where they could, and so increase their own opportunities in the region.

British Prime Minister William Pitt offered to return sovereignty of the Rock to Spain, if Madrid would assist in the recovery of Minorca from the French, for the loss of which in 1756, Admiral John Byng had been shot by his own marines on the quarterdeck of his flagship in Portsmouth harbour (on the rather spurious capital charge of not having done his utmost in the face of the enemy). The Governor of the Rock had reported to London that the place was just 'a source of expense, and as ill-adapted as the Eddystone Lighthouse [the original structure which had collapsed] for the repair of a fleet'.[16] On the other hand, if Great Britain's hold on Minorca was in doubt, then it was felt that Gibraltar must be held to maintain naval influence in the Mediterranean. 'To the possession of Gibraltar there are therefore great Commercial Benefits, as well as Military Splendour; the united consideration of which must at all times stimulate the Nation to preserve it as one of the most valuable appendages to the British Empire.'[17] In August 1759, the same month that the Battle of Minden was fought, Admiral Sir Edward Boscawen, operating with eight warships out of Gibraltar, freshly supplied and fitted out in the comparatively sheltered waters of the Bay, pursued a stronger French squadron westwards through the Straits, going on to burn or capture five of those ships in battle off Lagos in southern Portugal. Projection of power for the Royal Navy depended to a fair degree on having the use of secure anchorages at strategic intervals, and Gibraltar seemed to meet that requirement very well.

Minorca was returned to British control in 1763 at the Treaty of Paris, without London having to trade Gibraltar in the process. At about this time the Spanish Lines on the isthmus, with battery positions that threatened the town and anchorages, were further extended and improved. On the other side of the Neutral Ground there was comparatively little done for the time being. With the deep-water port at Mahon in Minorca once more open to the Royal Navy, the Rock correspondingly declined in perceived importance, and there was no real appetite in the Admiralty or in King George's Treasury in London to expend time, money and effort in improving the old defences. However, Lieutenant Colonel William Green (as he then was), had been tasked with carrying out a careful inspection of the defences in 1761. This Irishman, who had trained at the Royal Military Academy in Woolwich as a gunnery and engineer officer, had served with Wolfe at the capture of Quebec two years earlier. He applied himself energetically to the new task, and concluded that the defensive works were satisfactory in many cases, but that those of the Line Wall facing Gibraltar Bay, supposedly protected by the expanse of water, were too weak to counter a determined amphibious landing. Some of the battery positions were in a dilapidated state, and the stocks of ammunition and matériel held in the magazines and storehouses were inadequate, and in many cases of poor quality.

Green was appointed as Senior Engineer in Gibraltar, and continued to work to improve the state of those defences which had been allowed to become run down. He also suggested that a 'Company of Soldier-Artificers' be formed from suitable volunteers within the garrison, in place of the unsatisfactory hourly-paid civilian engineers who had been employed up to then and were not properly subject to military discipline. This new force was established on 6 March 1772; the successors of the Soldier-Artificer Company, who certainly were a significant improvement on the civilian workers, became the Corps of Royal Engineers. It took eight years to secure the necessary funds from London, but in 1773, the Deputy Governor of Gibraltar, Lieutenant General Sir Robert Boyd, was able to order the construction in cut stone of the new King's Bastion.[18] The work was constructed on the otherwise rather exposed West Front overlooking the Bay, between the Orange Bastion and South Bastion. This massive and formidable bastion commanded the whole foreshore from the Old Mole to the New Mole, and was armed with twelve 32-pounders and four 10-inch mortars, in addition to smaller pieces able to fire in enfilade along the shoreline. There were also bombproof casemates capable of holding 800 infantrymen in relative, if quite simple, comfort. This major work, completed in good time for the fresh outbreak of war with Spain, greatly improved the defences of the Rock against amphibious assault.

Somewhat to Boyd's disappointment, he was passed over and General Sir George Augustus Eliott was appointed as Governor of Gibraltar and commander of the British and Hanoverian garrison, on 25 May 1777. By coincidence, his uncle, Colonel Roger Eliott, had been the first British Governor of the Rock earlier in the century. The General soon found the defences to be still under-strength, rather more attention and money having been devoted to the protection of Port Mahon in Minorca. The civilian population, some 4,000 in all, many of whom would have no easy means of leaving Gibraltar, also had to be administered, sheltered, fed and watered at times of great danger. However, Eliott was in no way daunted by the scale of the task he had been set; he immediately began work to repair and improve still further the defences, and had garden plots laid out on the southern side of the Rock near to Europa Point, to try to supplement the rations of the garrison. 'No vigilance on my part shall be wanting,' Eliott wrote to the Secretary of State, Lord Weymouth, adding the caution that 'in case of service the garrison must be increased considerably, more than double the present numbers, especially artillerymen.'[19]

The Governor sent Colonel Green to London to request troop

reinforcements, and that the stocks of ammunition, stores, food and military matériel on the Rock be brought up to a proper scale. 'Our present store of beef, pork, pease, and butter is scarcely the complement for five months. Flour, biscuit, three months; oat-meal the same ... No time must be lost in forwarding the supply from England.'[20] Eliott's early training as an engineer and his careful study of the phases of war stood him in good stead. However, with British attention devoted to holding on to the colonies in North America, the provision of reinforcements and supplies was begrudged and slow in coming, and Eliott never had command of the 8,000 men he calculated as necessary for the proper defence of Gibraltar in time of war. He would have to place his faith in the natural strength of the Rock, in the abilities of his troops, and the skill of the Royal Navy, and may have been comforted to learn the sentiments of his rough and ready soldiery, expressed by Samuel Ancell, of the 58th Regiment of Foot: 'My religion consists in a firelock, open touch-hole, good flint, well rammed charge, and seventy rounds of powder and ball. That is the military creed.'[21]

War with Spain loomed nearer, and reports came in to Gibraltar of ships, men and stores being gathered in Cadiz, Malaga and Carthagena. As a result of Green's efforts in London, Eliott could feel some satisfaction that his magazines and storehouses had been, at least partly, replenished, and fresh troops had joined the garrison in place of those time-expired Hanoverian regiments who were anxious to go home. Some of the newly arrived units lacked both training and experience; the 72nd Foot, the Royal Manchester Volunteers, newly raised in the flush of patriotism that followed Burgoyne's unexpected defeat at Saratoga, required several weeks of intensive drilling in the shadow of the North Face of the Rock before they were considered fit enough to go on duty.[22] By contrast, the 39th Foot, which had been in garrison in the Channel Islands before being hurried to Gibraltar, had a reputation for steadiness.

Eliott was always concerned at the number of civilians on the Rock – unproductive mouths from a military point of view – that would have to be fed. The defences were in better shape, with the Grand Battery around the Land-Port Gate covering the Inundation obstacle, and the approaches to the Bayside Barrier and Forbes Barrier. The powerful Montague's Bastion covered the Old Mole (known as The Devil's Tongue) nearby. Willis's Battery was high up on the precipitous North Face, so that the Neutral Ground of the isthmus was well commanded by

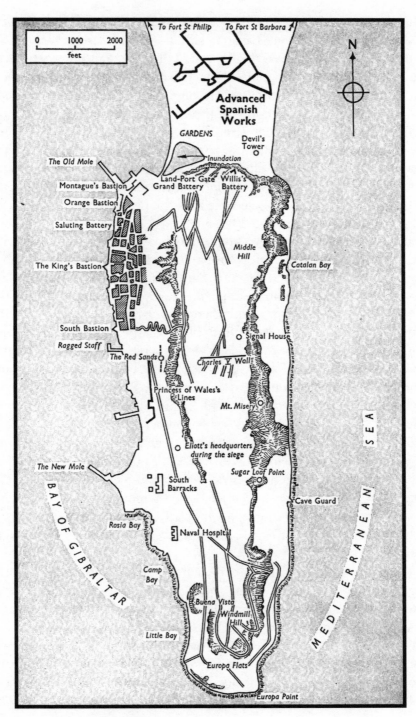

Gibraltar during the Great Siege.

Eliott's gunners. The front overlooking Gibraltar Bay now contained the new and formidable King's Bastion, with the Orange Bastion to the north and the South Bastion near the Ragged Staff to the south. From there an eighteen-gun battery supported the defences of a line-wall running southwards to the New Mole where there was a 26-gun emplacement, known as the New Mole Fort. All these batteries and bastions from the Old Mole southwards past King's Bastion to the New Mole could interlock their arcs of fire, and were able both to support each other and to sweep the approaches to the anchorages and landing points on which the garrison on the Rock would depend. A second set of defences, the Princess of Wales's Lines, occupied the higher ground near the Red Sands, and these also mounted heavy guns.

To the south of the New Mole, the three coves – Rosia Bay (the largest), Camp Bay and Little (Europa) Bay, were less exposed to Spanish fire than the anchorages to the north, and would prove useful as haven for the ships that kept Gibraltar supplied. Nearby were barracks, the Naval Hospital, and the encampment where the civilian inhabitants and the families of the garrison would find a kind of shelter from the Spanish bombardment as the siege went on. Even here, powerful batteries had been mounted to guard against any attempt at a seaborne landing, and Europa Point, at the southern extremity of the Rock, was also equipped with guns. There were some 400 artillery pieces on the Rock at this time, and over the period of hostilities this number would grow to a total of 663, including seventy mortars, some of them huge weapons of 13-inch calibre. There were so many guns available, that Eliott at times had difficulty finding enough gunners to man the pieces adequately. The almost sheer eastern face of Gibraltar was so impracticable for a landing in any strength that it could be left relatively unguarded except for a detachment at Sugar Loaf Point, but a careful lookout was always maintained.

The British had not taken care to secure the friendship and goodwill of the rulers of the Barbary coast, present-day Morocco. This was an astonishingly serious oversight. The Berbers had a long history of hostility to Spain, and frequent battles against the pirates sailing out of the ports on the North African coast had been a feature of Spanish naval operations for many years. The Sultan of Morocco might have been thought to be almost a natural ally of Great Britain. Almost all the food, fodder and fuel that the garrison and populace of the Rock required from day to day was obtained from Tangier and adjacent ports, and ferried across the Straits in swift small coastal craft. There was little fertile soil on Gibraltar to enable crops and vegetables in any quantity to be grown; some gardens and vegetable plots were laid out in the flat ground of the isthmus, but these surely would be unworkable once hostilities began. Yet, despite Eliott's demands that this source of supply should be secured by diplomatic means, almost nothing was done. The Spanish were more astute, and made haste to mend fences with their age-old opponents on the North African shore.

Captain John Drinkwater, who served throughout the Great Siege with the 72nd Regiment of Foot, wrote afterwards:

> In the early part of 1779, overtures were made by the Spaniards to the Moors, to farm [lease] the ports of Tangier, Tetuan and Larache. Of this General Eliott received immediate information, by a confidential message from the Emperor of Morocco … Since, by refusing to accede to their offers, he might subject his coast to be insulted, it would of consequence be prudent to arm his cruisers, in order to enable him to act on the defensive; he therefore requested that the English would supply him with naval stores for three new vessels … Such apparent disinterestedness, and so modest a demand, had a proper effect with the governor, who, considering the emperor's alliance of the first consequence to the welfare of the garrison, recommended to government to double the quantity of stores, that they might secure his friendship. Ministers at home, however, did not consider the alliance in the same light.[23]

The friendship of the Sultan was squandered by neglect, while the Spanish emissaries were active with their old foes, offering financial inducements if the North African ports would be closed to British shipping. As a direct result, the amount of valuable supplies brought in to Gibraltar from the Barbary Coast sharply dwindled in the months to come.

Poor diet, dull fare and a general lack of adequate provisions were always a pressing concern for any besieged garrison. Governor Eliott wrote to Lord Weymouth, soon after the commencement of the siege:

> It is believed Spain intends to prevent our Supplies; therefore all

sorts of Provisions should be sent at any Risk to make up a sufficient Stock for a year at least, besides daily consumption, and this for three or four Thousand Souls over and above the garrison, one half of which will labour or bear Arms, the Remainder cannot buy in Stock for subsistence [for] any Considerable Time.[24]

Throughout the whole of the Great Siege, the civilian inhabitants of the Rock, the 'useless mouths' as Eliott would so charmingly describe them, endured the miserable, cramped, conditions, the drab and meagre diet when ready cash was not available to purchase a few luxuries, the sickness and disease, and the dangers of what became a constant bombardment which, although it varied widely in intensity, rarely failed to maim and kill. No less than the British and Hanoverian soldiers and sailors who comprised the garrison and came through to eventual success and victory, their families, and the Rock's civilian inhabitants – men, women and children alike – who shared the ordeal, sustained the Great Siege as well.

Ironically, the negotiations for peace that eventually brought the Great Siege to an end in 1783 would again bring Great Britain to contemplate giving up Gibraltar, held with such effort and expense, if she could only regain Minorca and the fine deep-water anchorage of Port Mahon. This was seen as of more value to naval operations in the Mediterranean. After all, if the breeze was in favour, the current would carry ships through the Straits of Gibraltar, with faint chance of interference from the guns on the Rock, at least until the advent of long-range rifled artillery in the mid-nineteenth century (that same technical innovation, if employed from the Spanish mainland, would very quickly render Gibraltar untenable as a military and naval base). Therefore, in an age of smooth-bore artillery, Gibraltar was only of value to command the passage of the Straits while the Royal Navy could operate at will.

The Disagreeable Necessity

Those of Great Britain's colonial subjects in North America who took up arms against the Crown in April 1775 were matched to a degree by many of their neighbours who remained loyal and those cautious souls who were inclined to sit on the fence until matters became more clear as to who would be the winners. However, the British found that to suppress rebellion at such a distance, across the vastness of the Atlantic Ocean, was no simple thing, especially when there was a lack of appetite for the conflict, and the associated tax burden, in London. Military and naval operations were well under way by 1777, and proving indecisive – in fact, the American rebels were flagging, after a string of military reverses, when France, posing as their natural friend and ally but actually, and quite predictably, looking to gain from the situation, entered the conflict. In this way, the French plainly hoped to take advantage of their old rival's difficulties, and there was the intriguing possibility of reviving France's empire in North America. This military intervention would prove to be decisive in the conflict. Spain, on the other hand, with wide colonial possessions in the Americas, was reluctant to become involved, in case the contagion of colonial rebellion should be encouraged and spread with unforeseeable, and possibly uncontrollable, consequences for Madrid.

King Carlos III and his ministers attempted to play the rather spurious role of honest broker, professing themselves willing to mediate between the warring parties. The hope, apparently, was that in return for an advantageous settlement for Great Britain in her North American colonies, both Gibraltar and Minorca would be returned to Spanish sovereignty. The King's Ambassador in London, the Marqués de Almodóvar, was instructed to pursue the proposal vigorously. This was not a very realistic proposition, at even a casual glance, for if Great Britain could not win the war with the rebellious subjects with her own efforts and resources (and it was not yet at all clear that the British would not win), then no amount of mediation by Spain would persuade the successful American rebels to return to their allegiance to the Crown, just to suit Madrid. This was even more so after George Washington's successes at Trenton and Princeton in the spring of 1777, the unexpected local defeat of 'Gentleman' Johnny Burgoyne and his army in the woods at Saratoga that autumn, and the evacuation by British troops of Philadelphia.

On 6 December 1777 France acknowledged the rebellious American colonies as a sovereign state in their own right. The following February, treaties of friendship and defensive alliance were concluded with the fledgling American state, and in April 1778 a French fleet of seventeen warships, with 4,000 troops aboard, left Toulon bound for the Americas. The commander, Comte d'Estaing, had orders that he should only commence hostilities against the British once his ships were safely through the Straits of Gibraltar and into the Atlantic. The French force was shadowed by a Royal Navy frigate, and word was soon sent to London of d'Estaing's departure. Admiral Keppel then intercepted a French squadron in the English Channel on 17 June, although technically Great Britain and France were not yet at war and he was almost certainly exceeding his orders; this date, however, was generally accepted as that of the commencement of renewed hostilities.

Discussions between London and Madrid over the possibility of Spanish mediation in the war soon faltered, and relations between the two countries, never particularly cordial where Gibraltar was concerned, rapidly grew more sour. The British, unsurprisingly, maintained the right to treat their own colonists as they saw fit, regardless of foreign opinions or intermediaries. Carlos III cloaked his desire for an advantageous war in outraged declarations at high-handed British conduct, claiming to be offended by London's insolence, not only in spurning the, entirely fanciful, Spanish diplomatic efforts to achieve a settlement, but also over allegations of troublemaking in Spain's American possessions. Interference with Spanish shipping was also cited, a longstanding grievance over whether neutral vessels could justifiably be stopped by the Royal Navy on the high seas and searched for contraband goods being carried to and from enemy ports. No real complaint concerning the possession of Gibraltar and Minorca was raised at this time of rising tension. London had, in fact, been buying time with these discussions, and George III remarked in October 1778, 'I have no doubt next Spring Spain will join France. But', he added perceptively, 'if we can keep her quiet till then, I trust the British Navy will be in a state to cope with both nations.'[1]

Ambassador Almodóvar was withdrawn from London early in 1779, and on 12 April, France and Spain concluded in secret the Convention of Aranjuez, agreeing on a joint military strategy against Great Britain. France was mostly interested in prising loose the British grip on the island of Minorca, sitting as it did uncomfortably close to the approaches to the great naval base at Toulon, but also on recovering territories in the Americas, and expanding French influence across the Indian Ocean. Quite plainly, Paris had little real interest in just who was in possession of Gibraltar, other than as a means to exert pressure on British military efforts in other, more promising, theatres of war. Spanish attention, on the other hand, was firmly fixed on maintaining the security of her American colonies. While the safety of those possessions was paramount, and nothing would be done to put them in jeopardy, the opportune chance for the recovery of Gibraltar and Minorca was the spur that led Carlos III and his generals to war.

However, there was plenty of common ground between Paris and Madrid, and Louis XVI was bound by the agreement to carry on with the war until Spain had recovered Gibraltar. In the meantime, a joint French and Spanish fleet of sixty-six ships-of-the-line would be assembled in the English Channel under the command of French Admiral Comte d'Orvilliers, to support an invasion of southern England. The Royal Navy at the time could only muster thirty-eight ships under the elderly Admiral Sir Charles Hardy to oppose them. Committed to fighting several far-flung wars at the same time, and with very few allies, Great Britain was fearfully exposed to attack; the Militia would be mustered in the southern counties of England, and cattle, sheep and horses were driven inland, away from the grasp of invading armies.

Carlos III still had difficulty in finding a plausible reason to declare war, and so a rather feeble list of supposed British insults was drawn up – outrages against the Spanish flag, inciting rebellion in Spanish possessions in America, and a further 'insult' to His Majesty on account of the rejection by London of his efforts at mediation over the rebellious American colonies. The King, it was spuriously claimed, had no other choice: 'Under the disagreeable necessity of making use of all the means that the Almighty has given him, to do himself justice which he had in vain solicited.'² This was all just a thin pretext for war, a manufactured cloak of legality that fooled no one. Claiming 'noble impartiality', he may or may not have taken genuine offence at the rejection of his offers, and the fact that the British had declined them with polite expressions of the deepest respect for the King was conveniently overlooked. Carlos III was undoubtedly quite cynically hoping to take advantage of what was widely seen as British weakness at this time. Protests from London that his 'noble' offer of mediation was of no practical value or purpose, as the French also were very unlikely to agree to be bound by it, went unheeded. So too, was the British assertion that Spain's complaints were either groundless or had been settled by the payment of compensation to aggrieved parties. By then, of course, Spain had decided on war, and rumours to that effect soon spread.

On 25 May a motion of censure was brought before the House of Lords in London, charging the British government with wanton neglect over the state of the defences on Gibraltar, and failing to maintain an adequate naval presence in the western Mediterranean. However that may be, and the motion had as much to do with political point-scoring as improving Great Britain's military position, time was much too short to attempt any remedy with the scarce resources then available.

Early in June 1779 Eliott marked the King's forty-first birthday with a grand ball for the officers and their ladies, and review of the troops in Gibraltar. A full 41-gun salute was fired in celebration of the occasion, and among the guests were the Spanish Governor General of San Roques, Don Joaquin Mendoza, and his wife. A few days later, it was learned that Don Mendoza had gained promotion to the rank of Lieutenant General. Eliott naturally felt it proper to offer his congratulations, and with his senior officers in their very best uniforms, he rode out across the flat ground of the isthmus on Saturday 19 June, to pay a courtesy call. Don Mendoza, normally a most affable and hospitable man, was clearly ill at ease when receiving the British party. He tried to cover this with his usual courtesy, but was visibly embarrassed by the compliments and congratulations he was offered on his promotion. The meeting was unusually short, with almost no refreshment offered, other than a cup of hot chocolate for Eliott, and he and his officers returned to Gibraltar in a rather puzzled mood. Mrs Miriam Green, the chief engineer's wife, remembered, 'He did not receive them as he ought to have done, but seemed uneasy, the whole time they staid, which was not very long ... he did not even ask them to partake of any refreshment.'³ However, waiting for Eliott on his return to the Rock was Mr Logie, the British Consul to Barbary, with the information that a Swedish vessel had recently put into Tangier, carrying news that a French fleet had been sighted off Cape Finisterre, the twenty-eight warships under the command of Comte d'Orvilliers. He was waiting for the arrival of the Spanish squadron out of Cadiz, and it seemed evident that Spain was about to openly join France in the war against Great Britain. Don Mendoza must have been aware of this, which explained his being so uncomfortable in the presence of the British officers.

Spain had declared war on Great Britain three days earlier, when the Spanish Ambassador presented a list of impossible and implausible demands to the Secretary of State in London. On 21 June 1779 the communications between Gibraltar and the Spanish mainland were formally severed by Don Mendoza; the letters for the garrison and inhabitants, which normally came through San Roques, failed to appear and those sent out from Gibraltar were returned without explanation. British officers, who had been in the habit of exercising their horses on Spanish soil each morning, were politely but firmly turned back by the frontier guards. Soon afterwards, the small number of British families who had resided in San Roques were escorted, with those meagre possessions they could carry, to the Rock. Eliott received a letter from Don Mendoza, phrased in courteous and elegant terms, but saying that he had instructions from Madrid to blockade Gibraltar. 'Communications', Captain John Drinkwater of the 72nd Foot wrote, were

> shut with Spain, the guards are reinforced, and Grand Battery made into a Captain's Guard. The pickets are ordered to be accoutred with their arms loaded ... no one to remain in the Garrison but those who have property, or will resist in defending it ... The fortress became a little world of itself.⁴

A small party of British officers – Colonel Charles Ross and Captain Vignoles of the 39th Foot, and Captain Lefanue of the 56th Foot – who had been enjoying a shooting expedition in southern Spain – hastily crossed over into Portugal in disguise, and only got back to Gibraltar by rowing themselves in a small boat along the coast from Faro, dodging Spanish cruisers on the way, and making good use of the strong surface current flowing into the Straits from the Atlantic.

The population and garrison of Gibraltar had become at once entirely dependent upon the sea for their supplies and sustenance, apart from local fishing and the few meagre vegetables they could cultivate. Nothing, with a few notable exceptions, would be had from the Spanish mainland, and if the other supply routes – across the Straits from Morocco, along the rocky Portuguese and Spanish coastline from the ports in southern England, or from the British garrison in Minorca – were cut, the place would starve. The attitude of the Sultan of Morocco towards the warring parties could not yet be foreseen with certainty, but the outlook was not very promising. British neglect in not securing his support would have its malign effect surely enough.

> The town of Tetuan in Barbary, lying across the country behind Ceuta, was formerly the port from which all the fresh supplies were obtained for the garrison of Gibraltar, and for this purpose barks [barques] were continually employed going to and fro. ... Tangier, a sea-port to the westward, lying in the streights [sic], was, before the blockade, the port from whence the garrison was supplied with fresh stock.[5]

Carlos III's ministers had already taken steps to ensure that Mulai Sulaman, the Sultan of Morocco, remained outwardly neutral in the war, and they had succeeded so very well that the ports on the half-lawless North African coast would remain open and welcoming to Spain's captains and those of her French allies. By contrast, Great Britain would soon find there no neutrality at all, no haven, but those same harbours firmly closed to them, a strategic prize of considerable worth to Madrid. A real opportunity had been missed by the British. 'How great would have been our embarrassment,' the Spanish Prime Minister, Count Floridablanca, wrote, 'if, by omitting to form this connection in time, England had invited the Moors to attack Ceuta or Mellilla [Spanish enclaves in North Africa], or by piratical cruises in the Straits, to damage all our measures for the blockade of Gibraltar.'[6] If London had taken the trouble to make common cause with Spain's longstanding foes, how very different things might have been in the coming campaign – it is not overstating matters to say that the Great Siege of Gibraltar would have not taken place at all, other than as some half-hearted pretence. As it now was, little or no assistance could be looked for from the Barbary coast, and the future of the Rock would depend every bit as much upon the skill and valour of the Royal Navy as upon the fortitude and abilities of the beleaguered garrison of Gibraltar.

Eliott had civilian working parties conscripted and sent out into the Neutral Ground, to level the heaps of sand that might afford cover to any approaching Spanish infantry. No attempt was made to interfere with this work, even though the range was short, on the face of things a rather strange omission on the part of Don Mendoza and his artillery officers. However, Samuel Ancell of the 58th Foot suspected that a cunning plan was in preparation, and he wrote, 'We concluded that the enemy would endeavour to surprise the place.'[7] Meanwhile, not a great deal was happening in the Spanish lines, for the simple reason that Don Mendoza had been taken a little by surprise at the outbreak of hostilities, and some time passed before he could summon troop reinforcements and the additional ordnance, matériel, ammunition and stores, necessary for the conduct of proper siege operations.

The Governor had set his soldiers to improve the defences on the Rock, with large barrels filled with earth and stones chained together, and placed to add extra height to the battery positions and entrenchments. The garrison consisted of only 5,382 troops, almost all of whom were British and Hanoverian infantry, and certainly rather less than the numbers Eliott considered the necessary minimum for a proper defence. He had under command three small Hanoverian battalions, five British battalions, 122 soldier-artificers, and five companies of artillerymen (485 strong). The gunners had an obvious key role to play, but they were too few for the task at hand. So, on 3 July 1779, 180 infantrymen were 'volunteered' to be trained as gunners – 'ordered to join the artillery to be taught the practice of the great guns'[8] – a task that these soldiers accomplished rather well in the hazardous circumstances. The guard stationed at the Devil's Tower, a forward observation post on the isthmus, were now the only troops outside the main defences, as the Land-Port Gate next to the Inundation was firmly shut, as were the Bayside and Forbes Barriers on either side of the obstacle. The Devil's Tower, although apparently exposed to attack, was well covered by the fire of the guns in Willis's Battery, and could be manned without great risk for the time being.

Vice Admiral Robert Duff, in command of the Royal Navy's Gibraltar squadron, brought his flagship, HMS *Panther* (60 guns, under the command of Captain Harvey), the frigate, *Enterprise* (28, Captain Rich) and a sloop, *Childers* (12, Commander Pearson), from the Ragged Staff Bastion to close alongside the New Mole, a more sheltered position firmly under the protection of the batteries on the Rock. A part of Duff's squadron were still at sea, but some of his seamen, lacking active employment as the admiral seemed disinclined to go out and challenge the increasingly active Spanish gunboats, were put to good use in adding to the efforts of the garrison ashore, eventually being formed into a small and very effective marine brigade some 760 strong. Letters of Marque were offered to any captain of the vessels coming into Gibraltar so that they could legitimately attack French and Spanish shipping if they wished to do so, as privateers.

In addition to the naval and military personnel in Gibraltar, the civilian population comprised 3,201, of all ages, according to the most recent census. These were a mixture of 529 Britons, 1,809 Gibraltarians (mostly of Roman Catholic persuasion), and 863 Jews. There were also about another 300 'Moroccan labourers', who were considered, probably wrongly, to be unreliable and were encouraged to leave at the earliest opportunity. Eliott was as much concerned with the necessity to feed them as any likely threat they might pose to the security of the garrison.[9] Even so, the real problem that these civilian numbers posed was that, from a military point of view, they were almost entirely unproductive 'useless mouths', daily consuming the limited amount of stores of food on the Rock. Although the more able-bodied adult men could be put to use with pioneering and labouring tasks, they would – not surprisingly – try to avoid this arduous, and quite probably hazardous, service if they could. Soon, every ship and boat that set sail from Gibraltar carried a group of refugees making their way to safer parts.

The Spanish blockade of Gibraltar was still not complete – the squadron at Algeciras lacked real strength, and fire between the opposing forces had not yet been exchanged. This all changed on 5 July 1779, when a Spanish squadron of eleven warships, including two powerful two-deckers (both 74s) and five frigates, approached the Rock on a strong breeze from the west. It became evident that they intended to intercept a flotilla of three privateer cutters bringing munitions and stores for the garrison. A schooner, flying Portuguese colours as a ruse to deceive the approaching captains (Portugal was supposedly neutral in the conflict, but as so often was the case, Lisbon actively favoured the British over their Spanish neighbours), moved into position to head off the cutters, and in so doing came within range of the batteries on Europa Point, at the southern extremity of the Rock. The British gunners immediately opened a heavy fire on the schooner, which quickly wore round out of range, without returning fire, thus allowing the privateers to come into Gibraltar harbour unhindered. John Drinkwater remarked that this was 'the first hostile shot from the garrison'.[10] That night the British batteries were in action again, although this time they were firing on HMS *Enterprise* by mistake – her commander having decided against giving the agreed night signal to avoid alerting the prowling Spanish boats. Luckily, no hits were scored on the *Enterprise*, as she came into harbour from Tangier bringing Mr Logie back to Gibraltar with dispatches.

This action to ward off the attempt to interfere with the provisioning of Gibraltar was typical of Eliott's robust character, but it was a risk, as he had not yet received confirmation that hostilities between Spain and Great Britain had actually commenced. He was not one to suffer from doubts, and had made it plain from the outset that the British hold on Gibraltar was not to be doubted or trifled with. In any case, the confirmation of a state of war between the two countries was received the very next day, and Eliott had been proved to be right in clearing the way for the cutters to come into harbour. The pattern of operations for years to come was set in Gibraltar Bay and the Straits. There was skirmishing between coastal craft, and occasionally prizes were brought into Gibraltar, although Robert Duff missed the chance to intercept a Spanish convoy of sixty merchantmen on 11 July, watching the ships sail past but doing little to intercept their progress. It became evident that the Spaniards expected to starve out the Gibraltar garrison, and their preparations to construct additional batteries, parallel trenches and approaches on the isthmus proceeded at a rather languid pace. This was quite understandable for, on the face of things, it should be relatively straightforward to establish and maintain a tight naval blockade, using the many good ports and anchorages available to the Armada Espagnol along their southern coastline.

The squadron under Vice Admiral Don Antonio Barcelo, a tough and veteran naval commander, had taken up a position to impose a close blockade of the Rock. John Drinkwater recalled, 'The 16th [July] the enemy blocked up the port with a squadron of men of war, consisting of 2 seventy-fours, 2 frigates, 5 xebecqs and a number of galleys, half-galleys and armed settees [small lateen-rigged craft]; they anchored in the Bay off Algeciras.'[11] A close blockade of Gibraltar was said to be in place by 18 July 1779, and Drinkwater added that 'a small convoy of settees arrived at the Orange Grove [near to San Roques on the northern Bay-shore], laden with military stores, which the enemy began soon afterwards to disembark'. The siege and blockade were gradually gathering pace.

The Spanish attempts to maintain a tight enough naval blockade to starve Eliott and his garrison out were hampered by the perceived need to keep their main fleet concentrated in Cadiz. From there, the Spanish ships could get out into the open Atlantic fairly easily if a major threat developed. The blockading squadron based at Algeciras on the other hand, just across the Bay from Eliott and his garrison, was not strong enough to be effective at first, and had to operate in the fast-running waters of the Straits of Gibraltar, known locally as the Gut. Because it was susceptible both to the strong current flowing in from the Atlantic to the Mediterranean, and the prevailing westerly winds, handling the blockading squadron was tricky. It was not difficult to become out of position and laboriously have to tack back to the westwards, as Don Barcelo found on at least one notable occasion, when chasing a British privateer. Although he could deploy several of the powerfully armed and handy lateen-rigged xebecs, whose large crews could use oars if needed, the Spanish commander's concern at being out of position at a critical time was a continual and hampering worry. This exerted a persistent and worrying drag upon his operations. The Royal Navy had the same difficulty, of course, and the third of the great relief convoys that sustained the garrison was blown well to the east of the Rock, and took some days to claw its way back into safe harbour.

Beset with anxiety and indecision, Robert Duff was struggling with the enormity of the task he had been given. John Drinkwater remembered:

> So superior a naval force as the enemy now had in our neighbourhood alarmed Admiral Duff, who was apprehensive that they would make some attempts on the King's ships. Signals were therefore agreed upon between the fleet and the garrison, that in case the enemy should make an attack in the night, the

latter might afford the ships every assistance and protection.[12]

It was one thing to be properly concerned with the security of the ships when at anchor, but quite another to be transfixed with misgivings, as Duff seemed to be. His lack of initiative against Don Barcelo's squadron would soon become evident, and something of an irritation to Eliott.

If the garrison in Gibraltar was to endure, much would depend on the daring and skill of British naval commanders in the months to come, and on their determination to keep the Rock supplied. This was even more important once the ports of the Barbary Coast were shut to British shipping. At the start of the blockade Eliott had only forty head of cattle live and 'on the hoof' in the entire garrison, but he gave orders that enough should be slaughtered so that the sick could receive a regular small daily ration of fresh meat. Strict orders for the conservation of food stocks in public stores were issued, and as many as possible 'non-effectives' – wives, children and elderly and infirm civilians – were encouraged to leave, using the small blockade-running craft that made their way in and out of harbour. No direction was given about the private sale of food, and this, inevitably, caused difficulties when provisions were low, and only those who had the money could purchase a few longed-for luxuries. However, an experiment by the Governor, a vegetarian, to exist for a week on a purely rice diet of just four ounces a day, failed to impress the hungry soldiers or inspire them into following his rather austere example. Eliott did instruct his soldiers to stop powdering their hair with flour, as regulations still required, to conserve the scarce food stocks. Each horse's owner also had to have 1,000lb of feed in store for every animal, or have it shot or turned loose into the Neutral Ground. The Governor sacrificed one of his own mounts as an example to others, and stray dogs were ordered to be killed.

'Our Duty is hard,' Eliott wrote, 'but the garrison is in very good health; we have done much work, repairing old defences and constructing new.'[13] He completed the staff appointments – quartermaster-general, adjutant-general, the aides-de-camp, town major and so forth – necessary for the good administration and smooth operating of the garrison when under attack. However, it took time before these local appointments, which were, in effect, promotions with increased pay and allowances, were approved in London, where concern was inevitably felt at the associated increase in costs. Although these

officers held two appointments – on the Staff and at regimental level –
Eliott made it clear to them that they could not look to draw two sets of
rations, although in more normal circumstances they would have
expected to be able to do so.

The arrival of supply ships was eagerly looked for by the garrison, and
John Drinkwater wrote:

> A Venetian [schooner] arrived on 5 August, though fired at by the
> enemy. She (with the two Dutch ships who had brought rice and
> fruit) remained no longer than was necessary to take on board
> some of the inhabitants, who, apprehensive that the garrison
> would be besieged, thought it eligible to seek an asylum in time
> ... Scarcely a boat or vessel left the port without being crowded
> ... Early on the 6th, came in a Portuguese schooner from Tangier,
> with 44 buffaloes, 27 sheep and a few fouls [sic]; and two days
> following, another arrived with onions, fruit and eggs: the latter
> brought letters for the Governor, but no news from England.[14]

This last comment became a frequent complaint – 'No news from
England' – as the long tedious days of blockade, bombardment and siege
stretched first into weeks and months, and then years on end. The awful
dullness of isolation and repetitive routine while living on plain and
meagre rations, the constant tiring labour to improve and repair the
defences, all enlivened only occasionally by strong drink, bombardment
and fleeting moments of acute excitement and danger, would be among
the enduring memories of the Great Siege.

For the time being, the monotonous diet of official rations could be
relieved by catches of fresh fish from the rich waters around the Rock,
and Drinkwater remembered with some fondness that 'Turbot, salmon,
sole, hake, rock-cod, mullet ... mackerel are also taken in vast numbers
during the season, and shell-fish.'[15] The waspish Spanish gunboats,
astonishingly swift and strongly built craft, would shut off this ready
source of food supply soon enough, to the garrison's disgust at such
ungenerous conduct in harassing the fishermen. On 17 August, the
Spaniards tried to cut out a poleacre (a lateen-rigged craft similar to a
xebec) that was moored off the Old Mole. They were driven off without
too much trouble, but it was felt necessary to move all the smaller craft to
the less exposed New Mole to the south, as the activities of the gunboats
steadily increased. Soon afterwards, a rather enterprising trader,

ostensibly on his way from Algeciras to Ceuta on the North African shore, tacked and quickly put into the harbour instead, in a boat laden with onions and fruit to sell to the eager garrison. He also brought the interesting information that some 6,000 Spanish troops were now in the camp at San Roques, and that it was expected that this number would increase to 15,000 men before very long, with a grand assault made and the seemingly inevitable fall of the fortress coming soon afterwards.

On Sunday, 12 September 1779, Eliott abruptly raised the pace of operations, making it clear once again that any aggressive action by the Spanish forces would meet with a ready response. At 6.30am, as dawn sunlight flooded the hilly feature on the mainland known as the Queen of Spain's Chair, the British gunners on the North Face of the Rock opened a heavy bombardment on the Spanish siege lines. A 24-pounder gun had been dragged up the sheer rock face into position, and the first shot from the piece was fired by the newly-wed Mrs Skinner, whose husband was an officer in the Soldier-Artificer Company. The New Battery was sited some 900 feet above sea level (an elevation which made it almost impossible for the Spaniards to reply with any real effect, unless of course they used mortars), at what became known as the 'Rock Gun' or the 'Sky Battery'. 'At the first discharge our shot dropped short,' wrote Samuel Ancell,

> so that their advanced guards had time to escape to their lines, and their precipitate retreat almost occasioned a general laugh … When the enemy had reached their lines, we gave more elevation to our guns, and Fort Barbara and St Felippe received a heavy cannonade.[16]

A military band stood nearby rendering that stirring martial air 'Britons Strike Home'.[17] The firing continued all day, only ceasing with the failing light of evening. 'We kept up a very heavy cannonading for an hour … I never heard such a noise in my life,' Mrs Miriam Green wrote in her journal.[18] The guard in the Devil's Tower could not now be protected against attack, and they were withdrawn into the main defences. Eliott also had a company of sixty-eight marksmen, under the command of Lieutenant Burleigh of the 39th Foot, drawn from the most accomplished shots in each regiment and equipped with the most reliable muskets and best flints. This small corps was given the task to slow the work of the Spanish pioneers and labourers in their forward lines, and keep their outposts at a decent distance if they tried to come too far forward. Samuel Ancell remembered that the pace of activity certainly seemed to be quickening, and wrote, 'The enemy appear very busy; they are encamped at the foot of Santa Roque, to a great number, with some squadrons of horse.'[19]

This opening shot was to be the first major move in more than three long years of artillery bombardment and counter-bombardment between the Rock and the mainland. It seems that little real damage was done to the Spanish works that Sunday, other than to drive off some workers and foragers, and firing was soon suspended until movement was detected in their trenches and battery positions. The use of solid-shot was noticed to be rather ineffective, as the missiles were embedded in the soft sand with little lethal effect. 'Carcasses', hollowed-out shells filled with incendiary material, were also used, but proved only partly successful, as the Spanish soldiers found that they could quickly smother the burning bombs with sand as they lay still on the ground. Captain John Mercier of the 39th Foot devised a method for shortening the fuses in the $5^1/_2$-inch mortar bombs held in the magazines on the Rock, and this produced an air-burst effect when the projectiles were fired from the 24-pounders, causing considerable disruption and delay among the Spanish troops and workmen. 'This mode of annoyance,' John Drinkwater remembered with evident satisfaction, 'was eligible on several other accounts; less powder was used, and the enemy were seriously molested.'[20] Also in use were 'light balls', illuminating shells that were fired from 32-pounders to settle around the Spanish positions and light up the area during the dark hours. These were demonstrated to Eliott by Lieutenant Whitham of the Royal Artillery on 19 September, and it was noticed that the Spanish pioneers all stopped what they were doing and took shelter as soon as the light balls were fired. They were expensive and laborious to construct, and the besiegers quickly became used to them, with the consequence that they were used only sparingly.

The immediate effect of this bombardment was a noticeable slowing in the pace of entrenching work, and the placing of heavy guns on the isthmus. However, the Spanish gunners could be just as imaginative, and they also would employ air-burst shells in their bombardment, although their powder-filling proved of poor quality and often the projectiles did not explode at the right moment. This failing was noted with grim professional interest, and some satisfaction, by the British gunners. All this activity provided a measure of relief for the bored garrison, and the results of the gunners' work were eagerly observed, to such an extent that a Garrison Order had to be published on 31 October, that 'The service of the batteries is much interrupted by officers not on duty crowding upon them. Spectators are therefore desired not to go upon any part of a Battery from which there is firing.'[21] It was also found necessary to remind officers that strong spirits and females should on no account be taken into the battery positions. This was a prohibition that proved difficult to enforce, and ladies of easy virtue plied their ancient trade among the gun crews quite openly, and with a certain bravado, even when the garrison was under fire. Provisions had already begun to run low, and hoarding was on the increase. 'It is really grievous,' Samuel Ancell wrote, 'to see the fighting of the people for a morsel of bread, at a price not to be credited by those who never knew hardship.'[22]

In the English Channel, meanwhile, the combined French and Spanish fleet had assembled under the command of Comte d'Orvilliers, and a large force of French troops was making ready at Le Havre, Cherbourg and St Malo, gathering for an invasion of southern England. However, the two navies had separate operating procedures and signals, the standard of training was different, and the respective commanders found that working together effectively was altogether impossible, while disease ravaged their crews. The joint fleet had to put into Brest on 14 September during squally weather, and before long the Spanish ships were ordered south to Cadiz once more. The superficially attractive prospect of joint French and Spanish naval operations to dominate the Channel and threaten an invasion, in so doing crippling efforts to sustain the garrison in Gibraltar, would gradually fade away.

Vice Admiral Duff, commanding the Gibraltar squadron, had once been a valiant young naval captain, under Admiral Hawke, scouting the French naval bases at Brest and St Nazaire before the battle of Quiberon Bay twenty years earlier. Now, he proved to be neither energetic nor particularly enterprising. The Bay and the adjacent coastline were infested with Spanish gunboats and armed galleys, and it was frustrating for the garrison to have to watch in impotent disgust as blockade-runners laden with badly needed supplies were intercepted by Don Barcelo's boats. 'Our cruisers were under the necessity of returning to the Bay,' Samuel Ancell wrote, 'as the enemy were ever watchful of their motions, and our force is too weak to offer an opposition.'[23] Late in October the privateer *Peace and Plenty*, commanded by Captain McKenzie, came in from Minorca, chased by the ever-present xebecs. Driven ashore between Fort St Barbara and the abandoned Devil's Tower outpost, *Peace and Plenty* was eventually burned by the Spaniards. McKenzie and his crew made their escape into the defences of the Rock, although the boatswain was mortally wounded with a shot through the thigh. The captain brought news that the British and Hanoverian garrison in Minorca were in good health and spirits, but short of serviceable clothing and hoping to be resupplied and reinforced before very long. Eliott noted this, but he had difficulties enough of his own, and if Gibraltar could not hold out, then it seemed unlikely that Minorca would do so.

In addition to the fast xebecs, the Spanish gunboats, the jabecquillas, were particularly troublesome – fast, oar-driven and with a lateen sail, they were not so susceptible to wind and tide as the larger vessels in the Bay. Simply and robustly constructed, about seventy feet long and twenty in feet the beam with a heavy gun in the bows, each boat had a good turn of speed when the breeze was in the right quarter. These craft were a constant prowling threat to the survival of the Gibraltar garrison. 'The gunboats, in a calm, operated against our frigates by means of their oars, and were secure from pursuit.'[24]

Across the sands of the isthmus, meanwhile, the rather languid Lieutenant General Don Mendoza had been replaced as commander of the besieging land forces by Lieutenant General Don Martin Alvarez de Soto-Mayor, of whom great things were expected in Madrid. He was certainly more active, but rather rashly as it turned out, had offered to serve without pay until the Rock was once again in Spanish hands. De Soto-Mayor was still faced with the daunting practical task of feeding and maintaining large numbers of troops in a region with indifferent overland communications. This implacable logistical demand imposed its own measure of delay on the Spanish operations, but the preparations for the siege did progress, after a fashion, with the digging of more trenches and erecting new battery positions. Guns, munitions, stores and matériel were gathered around the steadily growing Spanish camp, situated just beyond the main fortified line that stretched across the neck of the isthmus from Fort St Barbara to Fort St Philip. Conditions in the camp were spartan, but the troops had a certain measure of freedom, and the officers and cavalry could exercise their horses in the adjoining countryside. They could also look forward to the comfortingly happy day when Gibraltar, once again, would be reclaimed for the Spanish Crown. Keen observers like John Drinkwater tried to calculate the strength of the forces being ranged against the garrison. 'The enemy's army, according to our intelligence consisted of 16 battalions of infantry and 12 squadrons of horse, which, if the regiments were complete, would amount to about 14,000 men.'[25]

The cramped, squalid, conditions on the Rock had the inevitable consequence of disease, and in time smallpox – horrible and dreaded – broke out among the civilian population, bringing with it potentially appalling consequences in the crowded garrison. The sick were sent into quarantine in the comparatively remote southern part of the Rock, to try to delay the spread of infection. Morale began to droop, tedium and bleak diet had their effect, as did the understandable desire to escape the scourge of disease. Numbers of soldiers began deserting to the Spaniards, singly and in small groups, making their furtive way across the isthmus at night, pursued by the musket shots of the sentries and picquets. When they were apprehended and brought back to the Rock, Eliott had the miscreants executed as an example to others, as was to be expected. This kind of ignoble traffic, in the other direction, with desertions from the Spanish forces towards what was evidently felt to be a preferable existence than remaining in the bleak trenches, would also be a common occurrence during the long months of the siege. In their camp, the spectacle of the hanging of deserters caught while trying to make their way to the Rock also became a common sight.

The Royal Navy squadron at Gibraltar was augmented by two small armed brigs, *Gibraltar* (12) and *Fortune* (10), and the frigate HMS *Porcupine* also came into harbour, but was in poor shape, having survived a lengthy battle with two of the deadly Spanish xebecs on her most recent cruise. Without this squadron, the Bay would have become simply a Spanish lake on which Vice Admiral Don Barcelo and his officers could operate at will, while the long western side of the Rock would be exposed to sudden naval bombardment and amphibious attack at any moment. Duff's lack of energy, however, meant that the British ships were not used to very good effect, and Samuel Ancell noted the watchful presence of the blockading squadron off Cabrita Point, writing to his brother:

It is currently reported that Spain's intention is, by famine, to oblige us to surrender; you may therefore conclude, that while the Enemy remains masters of the Straits of Gibraltar, our situation will be exceedingly disagreeable, and we shall be greatly necessitated for refreshments ... Barcello with the strictest vigilance watches the Gut, and some of his cruisers are mostly stretching from Ceuta to Cabritta Point ... Everything is getting at so exorbitant a price, that it is almost impossible for a person of moderate income to purchase what is required for sustenance ... We await the arrival of the fleet with impatience.[26]

At about 8am on 14 November 1779, lookouts on the Rock noticed sudden activity among the Spanish signal stations along the coast; this was correctly understood to indicate that a blockade-runner was approaching. Before long a privateer cutter, *Buck*, sailing out of Folkestone under the command of Captain George Fagg, was seen coming in from the west at speed with all sail crowded on. Don Barcelo's squadron, every one of the twenty-one vessels at their blockading stations, moved out to intercept the cutter, with the Admiral following in his stately flagship, *St Jean Baptiste* (74). The *Buck* soon came under fire, but Fagg tacked and sped away towards the North African coast, while the less handy Spanish ships, with shallower draughts, followed gamely enough, but were unable to sail as close to the wind as the cutter, and were forced to go eastwards by the strong surface current in the Straits. 'A cutter', John Drinkwater noted, 'or any vessel rigged in the same manner, from the formation of her sails can go some points nearer the wind than a square-rigged vessel, which advantage, on this occasion, enabled Capt Fagg to turn better to windward.'[27] The Spanish ships tacked also, and *St Jean Baptiste* wore round towards Cabrita Point to catch the westerly wind and run the *Buck* down. Fagg had also turned in the meantime, and slipped nimbly past the flagship, evading a rather ragged broadside from the Spanish vessel, and even impudently loosing off some shots from his small stern-chasers, to come safe under the guns of Gibraltar. Don Barcelo had to haul off to avoid the fire of the batteries at Europa Point; he had been outsailed by Fagg and left trailing behind, and this was plain for all to see. The safe arrival was greeted by the rapturous cheers of the watching garrison and inhabitants, whose rather drab existence had been enlivened by the dashing exploit.

The only damage done by the Spanish gunners was a round-shot through one of *Buck*'s boats. Duff had gone so far as to order HMS *Panther* to prepare to put to sea to aid Fagg, but then changed his mind and countermanded the instructions. This was probably right, for there was hardly enough time for his squadron to achieve very much, but it was typical of the Admiral's general inaction. *St Jean Baptiste* was forced eastwards into the Mediterranean by the wind and current like the rest of the Spanish squadron, a decided bonus for the garrison in allowing blockade-runners to come in from the Barbary coast in the meantime. Unfortunately, the *Buck* had brought neither supplies nor letters for the garrison, and Fagg was looking to replenish his own depleted stocks of food and water. Still, this neat display of audacious seamanship had been watched with great glee by those on the Rock, while Don Barcelo's squadron was well away from its proper station covering the Straits. Governor Eliott was sufficiently pleased with the exploit to reward each member of the crew with a crown piece from public funds.

The Spanish captains had to contend with the strong current to get back into position, and twelve valuable days were lost before the blockade could be re-established in any form. John Drinkwater wrote:

> Though our condition in the victualling office became weekly more and more serious, yet the Governor generously promised Capt Fagg assistance. What indeed could be refused to a man by whose manoeuvre the Port was once more open, and the Bay and Straits again under the command of a British Admiral? Only two or three half-galleys returned to Cabrita Point; the rest of the squadron were driven to the leeward of the rock.[28]

The Captain discreetly passed over the plain fact that Duff had done little to challenge the blockade. The Vice Admiral did consult his captains on the chances for success if, taking advantage of the situation, they set out to attack the Spanish gunboats still cruising in the Bay, or tried to cut out and engage the first of the Spanish ships that managed to crawl back into position while they were unsupported, but in the end none of this was attempted. Samuel Ancell noted that Captain Fagg had met other British blockade-runners on the way to the Rock, and had been warned that the harbour was closed tight by Don Barcelo's squadron: 'He asked if there was room for a coach and six to get in, which being answered in the affirmative, he rolled his quid [of chewing tobacco] two or three times ... and swore that he would get in.'[29]

For a short while it was easier for supplies to be ferried in to the Rock, although this valuable traffic had never ceased entirely, so enterprising were the corsairs and smugglers in the region. Huge profits were to be made for successfully landing a long-awaited cargo of necessities and luxuries for the garrison, and on 19 November a Moorish vessel put into harbour with a cargo of forty bullocks, fifty sheep and thirty goats. Despite their rather scrawny condition, they were a welcome increment to the stores of fresh meat in Gibraltar Town and were promptly sold at a good price. Other supply ships came safely into Gibraltar at this time, but shortages of all kinds continued to appear with worrying regularity. Inevitably, some blockade-runners were less fortunate, and the oar-driven Spanish gunboats were vigilant and continued to pick them off. This was all done in plain sight of the garrison on the Rock, and Duff's inaction to combat the Spanish blockaders attracted widespread notice and derision.

The construction of the Spanish siege batteries, both for cannon and mortars, demanded large quantities of matériel. The soft sandy under-soil of the isthmus had to be reinforced with large baulks of timber, and the firing platforms properly built up. This required, for each 26-pounder gun position, no less than six or seven lengths of timber each twenty feet long, and all this had to be brought into place across the poor roads of southern Spain or in coastal sailing vessels. The mortar batteries, because of the high elevation at which they worked, required even deeper foundations and yet more timber in their construction. The building of these works was hampered by the worsening weather, with the Spanish troops exposed in tented camps and incomplete entrenchments, in increasing discomfort. By a strange twist, deserters reported that fresh water was in short supply in the Spanish camp, and the soldiers were making themselves ill by having to drink brackish and partially saline water (just as they had done in the 1727 siege). The inevitable effect was to lessen morale and impair efficiency. 'This morning', Samuel Ancell wrote on 30 November,

> came in a deserter from the enemy and this evening another; they both belong to the Walloone Guards, and brought their arms with them: the latter was pursued by three horsemen, and would have been taken had not our people been very alert at Willis's by pouring grape-shot upon the pursuers ... They report that the

enemy are not to fire as General Alvarez is confident that famine will oblige us to surrender.[30]

Spanish preparations against the Rock were certainly measured, if not actually slow, and in part this was because Carlos III hoped to succeed in stealth, not by springing a surprise on the vigilant garrison, but by covert negotiation. The British, concerned at their lack of success in North America and at French advances in the West Indies, seemed inclined to compromise with Spanish demands. Approaches were made through diplomatic channels in neutral capitals, and an Irish priest, Thomas Hussey, and a playwright, Richard Cumberland, served briefly as rather improbable intermediaries between the Spanish and British ministers. The confidential discussions went on for some time, but eventually came to nothing, although their very existence goes a certain way to explain the apparently slack attitude among the Spanish commanders on land and sea in not pushing matters to a critical point at an early stage. Success might cost dear in treasure and blood on the battlefield, but be had cheaply by astute negotiation. What occasionally appeared to Eliott and his garrison as Spanish indolence or lack of spirit was arguably no such thing, but more a case of their opponents biding their time, while events took their shape elsewhere.

Governor Eliott would have been interested to learn that no overt effort was to be made to subdue the garrison on the Rock, at least for the coming year. This is clearly shown in a strategic plan of action for the French and Spanish forces, drawn up once it was realized that joint naval operations in the English Channel were unlikely to bear fruit: 'The project of a descent upon England is abandoned provisionally [but] to blockade Gibraltar, to have in America and Asia sufficient to hold the British in check, and to take the offensive in the West Indies.'[31]

Just before the end of the year, Captain Fagg took the *Buck* on a fresh breeze out of Gibraltar Bay, to the applause of the watching garrison, who had been so cheered by the audacious arrival in harbour a few weeks earlier. Fagg saluted Eliott by doffing his hat, before turning sharply away to the east to avoid the attentions of a heavily armed xebec that swept in and attempted to intercept his course. However, the good fortune of the *Buck* was at an end, for the vessel was waylaid by a French frigate while making for Minorca, and overwhelmed in a brief contest by massively superior weight of metal. Fagg was forced to strike

his colours, and the badly battered cutter was taken into tow by the
French ship, but foundered soon afterwards. This unhappy end for the
gallant little vessel which had brought such cheer to the Rock would of
course not have been known to the garrison in Gibraltar for some time.
December was a cold, wet, and miserable month – Christmas was a
sombre occasion, with belts tightened and prices rising, while Boxing
Day was more than usually wintry, with thunderstorms, lightning and
heavy rain damaging some of the newly constructed defences on the
Rock. An unexpected bonus for the garrison, quite apart from the fact
that the Spanish troops were also soaked by the rain in their camp
across the Neutral Ground, was that a large amount of debris brought
down by local streams at the flood was washed up on the shores of the
Bay. This provided a very welcome supplement to the dwindling stocks
of fuel on the Rock; coal was the most effective means for heating and
cooking, but every single piece had to be expensively brought in
through the blockade by colliers.

So far, the Spanish gunners had attempted little more than infrequent
shots to bed their pieces in and check the correct range, and to harass the
garrison outposts, but this was likely to change to something more far
dangerous before too long, once the better weather came. Samuel Ancell
wrote to his brother:

> The enemy began to fire upon our external works; they obliged
> the garrison gardeners, who work on the isthmus or neck of land
> (termed the Neutral Ground) to retire. Several Genoese
> fishermen who were dragging nets at the sea-side, were also
> under the necessity of retreating, leaving their nets, lines and
> tackle, on the beach … The enemy last night destroyed great part
> of our gardens, and unbecoming the character of warriors, they
> meanly stole the nets, lines &c that our fishermen left.[32]

John Drinkwater had already lamented the loss of the supply of fresh fish
due to Spanish action. Now, the distribution of food to those not entitled
to military rations had to take place under the watchful eyes of armed
guards to prevent disturbances. 'Many scuffles ensued amongst the people
on these occasions … The General ordered two sergeants, armed, to be
posted on each side of the door, and to preserve good behaviour among the
crowd.'[33] Hunger gnawed at the garrison and their families. 'Only think of
the Poor,' Mrs Miriam Green wrote in her journal, 'How Children Cry'd,

Mamma some Bread, and Mothers Wept when This they Said.'[34]

As the dismal year came to a close, some welcome additions to the rapidly diminishing stocks on the Rock were received when, as John Drinkwater remembered:

> The fly-packet arrived from Tangier, with forty goats, fowls and eggs, but no mail; this cargo, though trifling, was highly acceptable … A Neapolitan poleacre was luckily driven under our guns, and obliged to come in. On board we found about 6,000 bushels of barley … a cargo of inestimable value.[35]

The seaways into Gibraltar were precarious, but at least open for some enterprising captains, but – for all the imperfections of the Spanish blockade – Eliott and his troops, and the civilians alongside them, were plainly in difficult circumstances. The essential ability of the Royal Navy to sustain the Rock was about to be put to the test.

On 11 January 1780, the first battle casualty in Gibraltar was suffered, when a civilian woman was struck by a fragment of stone cast up by one of the ranging shots fired by the Spanish batteries. 'She was thrown down,' Miriam Green remembered, rather scornfully, 'and insisted upon it, both at that time and since, that it was the [cannon] ball that hit her leg. However, that was impossible as it must have broke her leg. She was more alarmed than any real hurt.'[36]

3

Moonlight Battles and Mountains
of Fire

On 27 December 1779, just two days after the Neapolitan trader was brought into Gibraltar harbour with its cargo of barley, Admiral Sir George Brydges Rodney weighed anchor in HMS *Sandwich* (90 guns), and set sail from Spithead in southern England.[1] Sixty-one years old, debt-ridden, gouty and irascible, Rodney had been appointed to the command of the Leeward Islands station in the West Indies. As Admiral of the White, Rodney was in command of a substantial convoy of the first importance, assembled to protect 300 merchant vessels bound for the West Indies, Portugal, Minorca and Gibraltar. Once additional escorts joined from Plymouth, Rodney had with him a substantial force, of which no fewer than twenty-one were ships-of-the-line, naval men-of-war with real force, together with twenty-two fast-moving frigates. He was attended by Dr Gilbert Blane, his personal physician, who had the task of keeping the ailing Admiral on his feet and fit enough for his command.

On 7 January 1780, when 100 miles to the west of Cape Finisterre, those ships intended for the Caribbean were detached under their escort, and Rodney pressed on southwards with the remaining transports bound for the Mediterranean. The very next day, Rodney's squadron intercepted a convoy of sixteen Spanish merchantmen, owned by the Caracca Trading Company sailing out of San Sebastian. Together with their armed escort of seven warships, they were run down and captured in a fine display of British seamanship. The great prize in this dashing action was the newly-built Spanish 4th Rate *Guispuscuano* (64 guns), which was promptly renamed HMS *Prince William* (Royal Navy 3rd Rate) as a compliment to King George III's youngest son, 15-year-old Prince William Henry (who subsequently became the Duke of Clarence and, eventually, the 'Sailor King' William IV), then serving as a midshipman on HMS *Prince George* (74).[2] The haul of stores in the

Rating for men-of-war in the Royal Navy, as in 1760

1st rate	100 guns with three gun-decks
2nd rate	90 guns with three gun-decks (90–98 guns from 1782 onwards)
3rd rate	64–80 guns with two gun-decks
4th rate	50–60 guns with two gun-decks
5th rate	30–44 guns with single gun-deck (frigate)
6th rate	20–30 guns with single gun-deck (frigate)

Smaller vessels, sloops, brigs, ketches etc., did not 'rate' a post of captain and would usually be commanded by a lieutenant or commander. The Royal Navy rating system changed in further detail in 1801. See N Rodger, *The Command of the Ocean* (2004), p. xxvii.

The Spanish naval rating system

1st rate	100–120 guns or more with three decks
2nd rate	80–98 guns with three decks
3rd rate	66–78 guns with two decks
4th rate	50–64 guns with two decks
5th rate	frigates, 32–44 guns, one or two decks
6th rate	corvettes, 20–28 guns, single deck

The French naval rating system

1st rate	90–124 guns with three decks
2nd rate	76–86 guns
3rd rate	66–74 guns
4th rate	40–64 guns
5th rate	frigates
6th rate	corvettes

captured transports was considerable, and had been intended to replenish the Spanish fleet in Cadiz, whose operational ability was hobbled, for the time being, by the loss. Those twelve ships laden with food and other provisions were sent on to replenish the hungry storehouses in Gibraltar, escorted by *Prince William* under the command of the newly promoted Captain Erasmus Gower, while the remainder of the prizes were sent back to England, with the glad news of success on the high seas.

Earlier in the month, unaware that Rodney was already at sea, Governor Eliott had written to Lord Weymouth, 'Not a vessel has got in here, the Spanish cruizers are so vigilant, consequently no supplies – many inhabitants near starving.'[3] Relief was near at hand; the brig *Good Design*, evading a prowling Spanish xebec, reached Gibraltar on the evening of 16 January not only with a welcome cargo of flour, but also the equally heartening news of Rodney's success off Cape Finisterre, and of the impending arrival of the additional supplies on the captured Spanish vessels. That was not all, for the frigate HMS *Apollo* arrived the following day with news of Rodney's even more remarkable victory at sea over a second Spanish squadron. Samuel Ancell wrote, 'The joyful and happy tidings of a fine fleet being within twenty-four hours sail of the garrison ... picture to yourself the joy of the garrison.'[4]

Shortly after noon on 16 January, the same day that *Good Design* reached harbour, Rodney's ships rounded Cape St Vincent, about twelve miles off the port beam. The topsails of a large force of Spanish warships could soon be seen on the horizon to the south-east by the leading ship,

HMS *Bedford* (74). This was the squadron commanded by 42-year-old Vice Admiral Don Juan de Langara, flying his flag in the *Fenix* (Phoenix – 80 guns). The Spanish Admiral had brought eleven ships-of-the-line and two large frigates through the Straits of Gibraltar from the Mediterranean, intending to combine forces with the Atlantic fleet under Admiral Luis de Cordoba y Cordoba, based out of Cadiz. Unknown to de Langara, de Cordoba had taken his fifteen ships-of-the-line back into port on learning of Rodney's approach, pleading as a rather feeble excuse the poor state of his vessels and a lack of supplies. As a result de Langara, outnumbered, now had to face a general sea-action without support.[5] His plight was made all the worse as he had lost contact with two of his best ships, the *San Genaro* and the *San Justo* (both 74s) in the squally weather, and had not used his accompanying frigates to scout ahead. Rodney could deploy eighteen ships-of-the-line to the Spanish commander's nine, and now de Langara had insufficient time or sea-room to avoid battle. Unless the rising seas and failing light intervened and forced Rodney to haul off, the Spanish commander faced defeat.

Rodney beat to quarters and all was bustle as the warships cleared for action. Despite the danger of running into shoal water along the looming coastline, he crammed on all sail and manoeuvred to get to the leeward of the Spanish squadron, so that de Langara could not easily run for the shelter of Cadiz, which lay about 100 miles to the south-east. Rodney was incapacitated with the agony of gout, and he spent much of the afternoon and evening in his cabin, directing the battle through verbal instructions passed to his highly capable Flag Captain, Walter Young. The hulls of the Royal Navy ships were now routinely sheathed with copper, and they moved more swiftly through the water than the unsheathed and fouled hulls of the slower Spanish vessels. 'Without them,' Rodney wrote afterwards, 'we should not have taken a single Spaniard.'[6]

Despite this, Young grew concerned at the delay in closing up to the Spanish squadron. He was labouring under the handicap of controlling the signals to the British ships, as they surged along through the rapidly rising seas, and at the same time conferring through runners with his irascible Admiral, who fumed in frustration at being confined to his cabin:

> I wished to have had the signal for a general chase, as night was coming on. This the admiral opposed and ordered the signal for a

line of battle ahead at two cables length. This I opposed, in turn, conscious that a great deal of time and distance would be lost.[7]

At Young's urging, at about 2pm, Rodney had the signal changed from 'Line Abreast' to 'General Chase'. He wrote in his dispatch, 'Perceiving the headmost ships very near the enemy, I made the general signal to engage and close.'[8] In this way, the British ships could 'run free' and get between de Langara and Cadiz; as Rodney's captains overhauled their opponents, the leading warship would engage the nearest trailing Spanish vessel of broadly equal firepower, with the other commanders moving past to engage their opponents in turn as they drew alongside. Rodney was aware that there would be a full moon that night, and as long as clouds did not obscure the light, the onset of darkness should not bring an end to the action prematurely. In the event, by 4pm, the Spanish squadron had been overtaken. The ships of Rodney's vanguard, *Bedford*, *Defence*, *Edgar* and *Resolution* (all 74s), were soon exchanging heavy broadsides with the Spanish vessels, whose crews undoubtedly fought well: 'The four headmost ships began the action which was returned with great briskness by the enemy.' Still, the Spanish rate of fire was noticeably slower than that of Rodney's gunners.

Within forty-five minutes of the opening of the engagement, Captain John MacBride on the *Bienfaisant* (64), drew alongside the two-decker *San Domingo* (70) commanded by Don Ignatzio Mendezabel. Both ships were firing rapidly into each other when the Spanish vessel suddenly blew up in a shattering roar of smoke and flame, briefly lighting up the darkening squally sky and casting a lurid glare across the turbulently thrashing sea and the battling warships. The entire crew perished in the explosion of the *San Domingo*, with the exception of a single Spanish sailor who was pulled from the sea, terribly injured, by the crew of the frigate HMS *Pegasus*. The man could not be saved, and died of his wounds soon afterwards. 'At forty minutes past four, one of the enemy's line of battleships blew up with a dreadful explosion; every person perished. At six pm one of the Spanish ships struck [her colours]. The action and pursuit continued with a constant fire.'[9] At dusk Rodney limped painfully onto the quarterdeck of *Sandwich*, which was just then coming into action, and ordered the signal 'Engage the Enemy more closely'. Turning then to his sailing master, Silas Hyslet, the Admiral commanded, 'This ship is not to pay any attention to merchantmen or small ships of war. Lay me alongside the biggest ship, or the Admiral [flagship] if there be one.'[10]

This tail-chase of the outgunned Spanish squadron continued without pause as night came on. The wind grew still stronger, but Rodney's captains ignored the dangers of operating in shoal water in such conditions. The Captain's log of the *Sandwich* read, 'Ran alongside the *Monarch* at $1/2$ past 1am, and poured in a Broadside, [both] great guns and small arms.'[11] De Langara put up a valiant fight, although his force was badly outnumbered, with the flagship, *Fenix*, exchanging shots with three British ships at one point. The main topsail of the Spanish vessel was shot away, and at 2am, the Admiral, who had been wounded in the thigh and forehead, struck his colours. Rodney had by then taken possession of six Spanish ships-of-the-line, in addition to the complete destruction of the unfortunate *San Domingo*. Four other warships, including the powerful *San Augustin* and *San Lorenzo* (both 70s), escaped in the darkness, although all with some damage, as did the two frigates, but the British ships were now in some difficulties, and Rodney had to get offshore, and out of the peril of running his ships aground. He remembered:

> Though the enemy made a gallant defence, ... had the weather proved but even moderate, or had the action happened in the day, not one of their squadron had escaped ... When the British fleet take the lee gage, the enemy cannot escape ... I am fully convinced that every ship of the enemy struck and would have been taken possession of had the weather permitted.[12]

Both *Royal George* and *Prince George* (74s) were signalling difficulties with the proximity of shoal water, and Rodney called a halt to the pursuit. Two of the prizes, *San Julian* and *San Eugenio* (70s), were, however, retaken by their Spanish crews in the strengthening gale that ensued, although the *San Eugenio* was subsequently driven ashore and broke her back. The Marquis de Medina, on the *San Julian*, had to insist that he be permitted to resume the command, as the small British prize crew under command of Lieutenant William, unfamiliar with the currents and reefs on that stretch of coastline, seemed intent on also running the ship onto the rocks. William was obliged to agree, and as a result the Royal Navy party was taken into Cadiz harbour, prisoners on board the very ship they had earlier helped to capture.[13]

Captain MacBride put a prize crew under command of a Lieutenant Lewis aboard the crippled flagship *Fenix*. Not wishing to expose the Spaniards to the smallpox suffered by some of his own crew on the *Bienfaisant*, MacBride gallantly offered de Langara terms for a remarkable parole:

> That neither [Spanish] officers nor men shall be removed from the *Phoenix* [onto the *Bienfaisant*], Admiral Langara being responsible for their conduct; and in case we shall fall in with any Spanish or French ships of war, he will not suffer Lieutenant Thos Lewis, the officer now in command of the *Phoenix*, to be interrupted in conducting and defending the ship to the last extremity, And if, meeting with superior force, the *Phoenix* should be retaken and the *Bienfaisant* fight her way clear, the admiral and his officers and men are to hold themselves prisoners of war to Captain MacBride, upon their parole of honour (which he is confident with Spanish officers is ever sacred). Likewise, if the *Bienfaisant* should be taken and the *Phoenix* escape, the admiral and his officers will no longer be prisoners, but freed immediately.[14]

The Admiral agreed the terms which, though not put to the test, would undoubtedly have been scrupulously followed. As for the destruction or capture of most of his ships, de Langara could claim, with considerable justification, that he had been left to face Rodney without adequate support by de Cordoba. His sailors and marines had fought well, and taken heavy casualties, but the foul unsheathed bottoms of their ships made them unhandy in the rising seas, and he had a hopeless task from the start.

Rodney, at the top of his aggressive form although gripped with gout, had seized every chance that offered to outsail and outgun his opponent, and had carried off a very clear victory. British casualties in the action were only twenty-two killed and 102 wounded, a number of whom were soldiers being taken to reinforce the garrisons in Gibraltar and Minorca, and who had been pressed into service as sharpshooters in the fighting tops of Rodney's ships – undoubtedly a novel experience as the ships pitched and rolled in the heaving seas. In his dispatch to Their Lordships in the Admiralty in London, the Admiral wrote that he could congratulate them on a signal victory obtained by His Majesty's ships under my command over the squadron commanded by Don Juan de Langara wherein the Spanish admiral and the greatest part of his quadroon were either taken or destroyed. The weather at times during the night was very tempestuous, with great seas making it difficult to take possession of and shift the prisoners of those ships that had surrendered to His Majesty's arms ...The gallant behaviour of the admirals, officers and men I had the honour to command, was conspicuous.[15]

Meanwhile, the garrison in Gibraltar still waited wearily for news. 'The weather on the 17th', John Drinkwater remembered

was very hazy; but clearing up on the succeeding day, one of the prizes [from the Caracca convoy] arrived without any opposition from the enemy. The Midshipman who brought her in informed us, that when he parted from the fleet on the 16th, Sir George was engaged with a Spanish squadron, and that just before they lost sight of them, a ship of the line blew up; but he was at too great a distance to distinguish whether she was friend or foe ... Our anxiety concerning the event of the action was, however, removed a few hours afterwards.[16]

The sloop *Childers* brought in word six days later that Rodney had moored off Tetuan, awaiting a favourable wind to come in. On 26 January, Gibraltar Bay was crowded with British ships of every kind, men-of-war and transports, as they came alongside Duff's moored squadron. Don Barcelo had prudently moved his own ships behind the shelter of a protective boom stretched across the part of the Bay adjacent to Algeciras, but HMS *Terrible* dragged her anchor and was taken by the current towards Fort St Philip. Shots were exchanged, but not a lot of damage was done on either side, although a Spanish prisoner on board the British ship was killed.

HMS *Sandwich* anchored off Gibraltar harbour, in company with the convoyed transports, the remaining captured Spanish prizes, and two xebecs that had been intercepted in the Gut by Rodney's fast-moving frigates, their national flags flying humbly below the ensigns of the Royal Navy. The captured vessels of the first action off Cape Finisterre were already there in harbour, together with the renamed *Prince William*. De

Langara, suffering still from his wounds, was taken gently onshore in a sedan chair, and, as far as was possible, comfortably lodged in the besieged town as an honoured guest. The Spanish Admiral was visited by Rodney when he came ashore on 28 January, when he was also introduced to Prince William. De Langara was suitably impressed to find that the son of the King was actively engaged in service with the fleet, with few, if any, privileges over his fellow midshipmen. Captain John Drinkwater wrote of the encounter:

> The Spaniard, astonished to see the son of a monarch acting as a petty officer, could not help exclaiming 'Well does Great Britain merit the empire of the sea, when the humblest stations in her navy are supported by Princes of the Blood.'[17]

The young Prince seemed to occupy his spare time on the Rock profitably, by touring the fortifications in company with Colonel Green. He made detailed sketches of the works, which he then presented to his father on his return to England as evidence of how well he had spent his weeks in Gibraltar. The Prince also went on a spree with his fellow midshipmen, visited the grog-shops in the town, became castaway with drink and got into a fight – all in all, not a bad apprenticeship for a future king.

The opportunity was now taken by Eliott and Rodney to secure the release of British prisoners languishing in Spanish gaols, but Lieutenant General de Soto-Mayor needed some persuasion to co-operate. Frustrated, Rodney was quite ready to re-embark the senior Spanish officers and take them back to England, and he wrote to the convalescent de Langara:

> The release of himself and the Spanish officers entirely depends upon Spain's immediately releasing all British prisoners of war now in her power. An equal number of prisoners shall be returned for those sent by Spain. Humanity obliges the admiral [Rodney] to offer those prisoners who are now sick, if they may be received by the Spanish general, but this shall be the last time, unless an exchange takes place.[18]

Such a magnanimous gesture, of course, also had the benefit of transferring the cost and inconvenience of caring for the sick and wounded prisoners back to the Spanish authorities. Soon afterwards, de

Langara and his officers were sent to the mainland on parole not to serve against Great Britain again until formally exchanged. Among the British prisoners released at this time was young Lieutenant William, who had gone aboard the *San Julian* with a prize crew after the Moonlight Battle, but had to yield the command as the ship ran into shoal water. When leaving, one of the paroled Spanish officers looked back, and gesturing at the massive North Face of the Rock, said to the soldiers escorting the party, 'Give up that to us and all will be well.'[19] Not surprisingly, this produced nothing in return but smiles. The good treatment given to de Langara and his captured crews impressed the Spaniards, and their own treatment of British captives, which had up to then been brusque enough to prompt protests from Eliott, improved noticeably.

Before those ships intended for the resupply of the British garrison in Minorca left Gibraltar, Eliott removed the 73rd Foot (2nd Battalion, MacLeod's Highlanders, raised in the Highlands and over 1,000 men strong, under the command of Lieutenant Colonel the Honourable George McKenzie) to augment the garrison on the Rock. The regiment had served on deck and in the fighting tops as marines in the recent naval actions, and had four men killed on board HMS *Defence*. Although Minorca was also under threat, Eliott had the authority to keep the 73rd in Gibraltar, and they were a welcome addition to a garrison weakened by sickness and the daily trickle of casualties and injuries. The newly arrived troops reputedly wore the kilt, which would have lent a little colour to their otherwise rather drab surroundings. Of rather more practical consideration were the stores in the captured Spanish ships that could have legitimately have been sold to the highest bidder, according to the conventions of the time, but Rodney was aware of how pressing the garrison's needs were. The Admiral gave orders that they should not be sold openly, and Eliott wrote to him in appreciation:

> You are pleased, with the universal consent of the captors, to make me a tender thereof for His Majesty's service, at a price to be fairly adjusted in preference of every other consideration. I accept with the utmost gratitude and thanks this very generous and noble proposal of so much importance to His Majesty's service in our present situation.[20]

The offer was all the more remarkable as Rodney had quite a reputation for avarice, being notoriously prone to getting into debt, and not very good with money. Another additional increment for the garrison supply stocks was the safe arrival of a transport carrying a large cargo of salted Newfoundland cod, which Eliott immediately bought with public funds. However, this proved to be rather drab fare and was unpopular with the soldiers and civilians alike, however tight their belts might have become.

Those ships destined for Minorca sailed under escort of HMS *Marlborough* and *Invincible* on 31 January. The *Childers* also got away through the Gut, at the second attempt, taking dispatches from Eliott and Rodney back to London. News of the victory over de Langara's squadron had reached London first of all through the British Ambassador in Brussels, who had sight of an entirely false Spanish dispatch foolishly claiming a resounding success at sea. Very few were deceived, and Rodney's own account of the action, when it arrived, set any doubts at rest. Robert Duff, once a dashing frigate captain, but now tired and disappointed, went back to England as the fleet departed on the evening of 13 February. So too did many of those soldiers' families who could not 'show' twelve months' store of food with which to sustain themselves (calculated as either 250lb of flour or 360lb of baked biscuit). 'I shall send home with the transports all useless mouths amongst which many women and children,' Eliott wrote in his dispatch to London.[21] The Gibraltar squadron now came under the command of Commodore Eliott (no relation to the Governor), who hoisted his broad pennant on HMS *Edgar*, which had been detached by Rodney as her crew was reduced by sickness. Eliott also had the two-decker *Panther*, the frigates *Porcupine* and *Enterprise*, and the sloops *Fortune* and *Gibraltar*.

Rodney's success in resupplying the Gibraltar garrison in this way so comfortably replenished Governor Eliott's stocks that he probably now had more supplies than at the commencement of hostilities. 'Our stores and magazine were full,' Drinkwater wrote, adding with unintentional humour, 'and new spirits were infused into the troops.'[22] Such optimism was premature, and the activities of the blockade-runners from Barbary suddenly tailed off, as the supplies they carried no longer commanded the good prices necessary to make the hazardous trips worthwhile. The valuable activities of these enterprising traders would be missed, and the traffic never recovered its previous volume. The stocks of gunpowder brought ashore from the captured Spanish ships were also taken into use on the Rock, but found to be of inferior quality and not really fit for service except in an emergency.

Rodney was suffering from a severe head-cold at this time, and was glad to leave the Rock and get out into the open waters of the North Atlantic. His success over de Langara's squadron, and the first major resupply of Gibraltar, naturally depressed spirits both in the camp at San Roques and in the Council of State in Madrid. The inability of the Spanish naval commanders to properly co-ordinate their efforts was evident, and the chances for success against Eliott and his garrison suddenly appeared to have become slim. Still, within a few days of Rodney and his squadron leaving the Straits, their passage marked by signal rockets fired from the observation posts along the Spanish coastline, Don Barcelo had re-imposed the close blockade of the Rock once more. Then Admiral de Cordoba slipped out of Cadiz and intercepted a large British convoy off the Azores, bound for the East Indies but inadequately escorted and soon taken captive. No fewer than sixty-five prizes were triumphantly brought back into Cadiz laden with valuable cargoes, all of which seemed suddenly to brighten Spanish prospects for the continuing operations. Meanwhile, the British government was beset by other troubles, such as the sudden outbreak of the anti-Catholic Gordon Riots in London, which paralyzed the capital for several days in conditions not unlike civil war, requiring the deployment of troops to restore order. This together with the loss of the Indies convoy and the continued lack of success in America seemed to point to a very clear overstretching of military and naval capability.

In a fresh attempt to negotiate a submission by Great Britain, an offer would soon be made that if Gibraltar was given up, on the pretence that the garrison had been starved out and had no choice but to submit, Eliott and his troops would be permitted to withdraw with all military honours. Any stores left in place would be purchased at a good price, and compensation paid to the British Treasury for the cost of having to improve the defences as tension with Madrid rose. Furthermore, Spain would end its alliance with France, and encourage Louis XVI to stop supporting the American rebels. This offer, almost fanciful in ambition and scope, and assuming far more than could possibly be performed, was seen to be impractical and nothing came of it. In the meantime, the Spanish troops in camp beneath the Queen of Spain's Chair were observed to be at exercise, and performing manoeuvres and sham attacks, while pioneers and labourers worked on extending and improving the siege lines and battery positions.

The Sultan of Morocco, almost ignored by Great Britain still, had been persuaded by Spain to withdraw protection from all shipping using his ports. This was of no particular concern to the Spanish and French, whose captains had the use of numerous safe harbours on the long southern Spanish coastline, unlike their British counterparts, who had to operate far from home ports and with the Bay of Gibraltar closely blockaded by Don Barcelo and his squadron. It also exposed British shipping to attack while they were in the Sultan's ports, as the Spaniards were assured that little or no action would be taken against them if they did so. This apparently even-handed course of action, with the superficial outward appearance of impartiality towards the warring parties, was the beginning of a hardening of attitude and increasing hostility by the Sultan towards British vessels and interests. 'The Emperor of Morocco first offered these ports to the English, on the same terms granted to the Spaniards ... All along the sea coast of Barbary, Algiers, Tunis etc., the English are preferred.'[23] That goodwill had been squandered, and the opportunity to make common cause against the Spanish allowed to go begging. So much, then, was missed and put at risk by this neglect in British diplomacy.

By the early summer, the euphoria felt in the garrison at the arrival of Rodney's supply convoy had faded. The blockade had been re-imposed and Eliott was once more expressing his concern at the effects of the attentions of the Spanish xebecs, and their equally dangerous smaller cousins, the fast jabecquilla gunboats. Vessels that left Gibraltar were still encouraged to take away more of the 'useless mouths' of the civilian population, to allow the meagre supplies to be eked out; the salt-fish was being issued, but this was less welcome than beef or mutton, and was thought to induce scurvy. Those few vegetables that were available were stale and unappetizing, and there was little opportunity now to go out into the garden allotments of the isthmus. Dreaded smallpox had appeared, but austere Eliott refused, apparently as a matter of conscience, to permit the doctors to inoculate. 'Smallpox raging very bad', Miriam Green wrote in her journal, 'children dying every day ... It is to be wished inoculation had been allowed.'[24] The disease, it was widely believed, had been brought to Gibraltar aboard Rodney's ships, and the account of the arrangement over the manning of the captured Spanish flagship *Fenix* supported that idea. However, the celebrations for the King's birthday on 4 June were again punctiliously observed, with the discharge of a 42-gun salute. Meanwhile, news came in from Mr Logie in Tangier that the Spaniards were preparing a fire-ship attack on Commodore Eliott's squadron, and on the moorings and harbour facilities alongside the Rock. Despite receiving this useful inform-ation, Don Barcelo's next move seemed to come as something of a surprise to the garrison.

Just after 1am on Wednesday, 7 June 1780, the officer of the watch on board HMS *Enterprise*, anchored at this time just off the New Mole, was alerted by shouts from lookouts in the guard-boats to the sight of spread sets of sails, becoming dimly visible through the haze and mist across the Bay to the west. A hail was given, but this met the rather improbable shouted response that they were bringing in a cargo of fresh beef from Morocco. A second hail met with no answer, and the alarm was given – three signal guns were fired in quick succession by *Enterprise* to alert the other ships in the harbour and the garrison ashore. The mysterious vessels were Spanish fire-ships, nine of them, making use of the moderate north-westerly breeze to bear down on the British anchorage. Almost immediately, the ships began to spout flames and showers of sparks as the scratch Spanish crews set light to the combustibles, fire-pots, stacked timber and tar barrels packed tightly on board, before taking to the boats and rowing hard away from danger. Three of the leading ships were chained together in a rough crescent formation, intended to increase the chance of catching one or more of the moored British vessels in their fiery embrace. They resembled 'moving mountains of fire, I was actually stupid with fright', Mrs Miriam Green wrote afterwards of the scene.[25] The whole of the western side of the Rock was vividly lit up by the flaming and sparking vessels, as the sails and standing rigging caught alight, the spurting flames leaping from yard to yard with terrifying speed.

Captain Lesley, on board *Enterprise*, ordered the anchor cables to be cut, so that his ship could move closer inshore and avoid the blazing 'Hell-Burners', but this was not done before some intrepid Spanish seamen and marines managed to heave fire-pots and grenades onto the upper deck of the frigate, and then made off in their boats. These missiles were swiftly extinguished by Lesley's crewmen with little damage done. The garrison was now thoroughly alerted, and the 32-

pounder batteries on the New Mole began to fire bar-shot at the closest of the fire-ships to divert them from the anchorage; the gun-crews on *Panther* engaged them at the same time, with carefully aimed shots as they drifted down towards Rosia Bay. 'The guns from all the batteries in the garrison that could bear on them joined likewise in the discharge.'[26] This cannonade seemed to slow the ships, the breeze lessened and the current began to take them southwards along the western side of the Rock and out of harm's way. Longboats manned with sailors also put out from the anchorage to close with the blazing vessels, throwing ropes with grappling irons to hook on and tow them away to the south where they could do least harm. This was done at considerable risk, as there was an often-used technique of planting barrels of gunpowder deep in the holds of fire-ships intended to detonate at the last moment, when closest to their intended targets. This did not happen, perhaps because of the faulty quality of the Spanish stocks of powder, but the British sailors in their scorched longboats could not know with certainty that this was so. As it was, one by one, the burning vessels passed safely by, and the Gibraltar squadron and the shipping in the harbour were safe for the time being.

The fire-ship attack should not have been unexpected, as the garrison had received information from Mr Logie and others that such an effort was being prepared. There had been an earlier attempt, but the wind dropped at the last moment, and it had all come to nothing. Although the second attack had failed, it had been a well-handled operation on the whole, and was really only foiled by the prompt and robust reaction of the boat-crews from the ships in the harbour, whose efforts to tow them away were carried out at such great risk, and of the gunners on the Rock. John Drinkwater wrote that the sailors who grappled with the fire-ships and dragged them away

> cannot be too highly commended for their courage, conduct and alertness. Their intrepidity overcame every obstacle and although three of the ships were linked with chains and strong cables, and every precaution taken to render them successful, yet, with uncommon resolution and activity, the British seamen separated, and towed ashore, the vessels, with no injuries to themselves other than a few bruises.[27]

Even so, one of the fire-ships passed so close to HMS *Panther*, anchored in Rosia Bay, that the pitch caulking on her sides was melted in the fierce heat; the terrible fear of wooden vessels and fire at sea was almost a reality for Eliott's squadron that night.

> Captain Brown, of the *Fortune* sloop, then at anchor off the New Mole, happening this night to be on shore from his vessel, in order to avoid any censure that might arise on account of his absence at such a crisis, and eager to get to his sloop, none of the gates being left open at night, and having no permit to procure the opening of them, nor the letting down of the drawbridge, took a desperate leap over the line-wall, which is at least forty feet high from the stony shore below, and swam to his vessel.[28]

Two of the blazing fire-ships drifted off out into the Straits, where Don Barcelo's blockading squadron had taken up station, hoping to intercept any British vessels that might be driven out of the anchorage by the attack. The other seven ships grounded on the rocky shoreline, where they blazed on for a long while, until rain began to fall with the growing light of the new morning. 'They burnt with surprising fierceness for three hours, the masts of some stood to the last, and appeared as under sail … the terrified inhabitants, together with the women and children, were wringing their hands.'[29] The two larger ships, one of about 700 tons, smouldered on all that following day despite the rain – the wrecks were eventually broken up by the garrison to use as firewood: 'Instead of inflicting the least damage to the stores or shipping of Gibraltar, they only served to increase our small stock of fuel.'[30] Firewood was always in short supply, and the colliers that had been intended to bring fuel for the garrison had been too late in coming to join Rodney at his rendezvous in January, and had missed the convoy. The fire-ship attack, accordingly, paid an unexpected bonus to the garrison.

Although no serious damage had been inflicted on Eliott's defences or on the British ships in the Bay, the attack had come close to success, as was shown by the peril in which *Panther* had stood at one point. The twenty supply ships at anchor at New Mole Head, in particular, had been in danger and would have been a serious loss if the fire-ships had got to them. But for the north-westerly breeze dropping at a certain moment, and the prompt action by the British gun and boat crews, things might have been much worse for the anchorage, and the rather exposed main powder magazines for the garrison and the essential storehouses, in plain sight of the Bay.

There was some surprise that the attack had not been supported by the Spanish shore batteries and the usually active and dangerous gunboats cruising in the Bay, but this was just one of several occasions when the various arms that could be deployed against the Rock were not used together to any real effect. The Spanish artillerymen, in fact, had been standing ready at their pieces, but for some inexplicable reason, the order to commence firing never came; Eliott learned this from a deserter who came across to the garrison a short time later. It was certainly odd, but the harassed inhabitants in Gibraltar Town, many still in their night-clothes and anticipating just such a bombardment, had run through the glaringly illuminated streets, seeking the greater protection of the southern parts of the Rock. In the midst of all the night's excitement, a small supply schooner from Tangier managed to make its way, unnoticed and unmolested by either Spanish gunboats or British batteries, into Gibraltar harbour with a welcome cargo of chickens and hides, the latter commodity desperately needed to replace the rotten footwear of the garrison.

An inevitable result of the failed fire-ship attack, of course, was to encourage and lift the morale of the garrison. While the probes conducted by the gunboats remained a constant irritation, the other Spanish naval operations were not very successful, on the whole. HMS *Panther* and *Enterprise* were attacked by night on 24 June by two frigates, a xebec, a galley and some jabecquillas, and a resulting accidental explosion on board *Enterprise* injured fifteen seamen. *Panther* was attacked again in Rosia Bay three nights later by gunboats which also engaged the adjacent shore batteries at the New Mole. This caused a lot of alarm, as it was believed that another fire-ship attack was in preparation, and the populace of Gibraltar Town fled to the southern end of the Rock once again. These exchanges had little point, other than as nuisance activity, although they did serve to keep nerves, particularly of the civilians on the Rock, at a stretch. Eliott had initially welcomed the presence of the naval vessels alongside Gibraltar harbour, able to add the weight of their own massive broadsides to that of the defence, but the warships were not being used in any really aggressive manner to establish local superiority over the

Spanish ships and gunboats in the Bay itself. Commander Eliott could argue, with a degree of truth, that his small force had insufficient numbers to make such an effort a very realistic prospect. However, there was the ever-present danger of one or other of the warships catching fire with potentially catastrophic consequences for the adjacent batteries and powder magazines on the Rock, in much the same way of a successful fire-ship attack. 'If the magazines blow up we all go with them,' the Governor wrote pointedly.[31]

It increasingly seemed that *Panther* was serving little useful purpose, other than as a convenient target for Spanish attacks. Accordingly, early in July, she set sail for England under command of Captain Harvey, carrying about 100 seamen who had been captured aboard the privateer *Admiral Keppel*, and recently released from captivity in Spain. It appears that their physical state was not good enough for them to provide a useful reinforcement for the marine brigade on the Rock. The steadily worsening tally of sickness among the garrison, their families and the remaining civilians was of growing concern, a combination of the monotonous and unhealthy diet, and the increasingly unsanitary conditions in the town. The toll taken can be seen in the simple fact that by August 1780, some 500 had died of smallpox alone. Children were dying at the rate of twenty each week, and Miriam Green's daughter, Charlotte, caught the disease but recovered, unlike the family's maid. In her anxiety and anguish, the engineer's wife uncharitably, but with real bitterness, suspected Governor Eliott of not regretting the loss of life, lessening as it did the numbers of 'useless mouths' that had to be fed from steadily declining stores. 'A great Person', she wrote, 'in the garrison says – He thinks it a fortunate Circumstance to those Soldiers who have large familys to lose three or four Children.'[32] The hot weather, often with still and stifling air brought in by the dry easterly wind known as the 'Levanter', made life ever more oppressive; tempers were short, and the outlook seemed to be bleaker with every week that passed.

The tedium may have helped to bring on a sharp feud between the Deputy Governor in Gibraltar, Sir Robert Boyd, and Colonel Charles Ross, the Commanding Officer of the 39th Foot. Boyd was also the Colonel of that Regiment, and there was evidently some ill-feeling between the two men.[33] The problem seemed to arise from the question of who was to take the parade of the regiment at the regular reviews conducted by the Governor to maintain smartness and efficiency among the garrison. On some occasions both officers would turn up, and on others neither would do so, leaving the second-in-command, Major William Kellett, to take the parade in their absence after waiting in vain to see who would appear. It all seemed very foolish, and the matter came to a head at a parade on 23 August, with Ross referring to Boyd disrespectfully as a 'storekeeper', in front of the assembled troops, and the 39th nothing but a 'storekeeper's regiment'. Miriam Green wrote of the extraordinary incident:

> Colonel Ross went there under a visible agitation: after the Regiment was Drawn up he asked if General Boyd as Commanding Officer of the 39th was upon the Parade. He was told Not. He then ordered the Articles [of War, read so that the men were reminded that they were under military discipline] to be Read, after which to the surprise of everybody he addressed the officers and soldiers talking first of the True Meaning of the Articles, and afterwards attacking the Colonel of the 39th calling him Bob Boyd, and the Regiment the Storekeepers Regiment ... He also ordered the Adjutant to tell the General all he had been saying! But as he declined to do it one of the General's a.d.c's did.[34]

Boyd's military career had begun as a commissary officer in Minorca, which Ross appeared to think a menial role. Boyd had him put under arrest and a court martial was convened under Colonel Green, which resulted in Ross being suspended from duty for twelve months for gross insubordination – part of his emphatic defence, according to Mrs Green, was that 'General Boyd had been a storekeeper.' Eliott promptly commuted most of the sentence, in the process causing some indignation in the 39th Foot, whose sense of honour had been so carelessly slighted, but the Governor could not lightly lose the services of such a talented, if argumentative, officer as Ross at a time when the pace of the Spanish operations was quickening at last.

Colonel Charles Mawhood, commanding officer of the 72nd Foot, the Manchester Volunteers, died on 29 August 1780, in agony because of the stone (one piece, the size of a pistol-ball, was taken from his kidney at the autopsy). This gave Eliott the chance to transfer Charles Ross to that regiment, where he could be useful and make less mischief. Ross was confirmed in the command of the 72nd Foot towards the end of the year, once approval for the transfer was received from London. He was also restored to favour within the garrison remarkably quickly, receiving brevet rank as Brigadier General, and made the commander of one of the most successful offensive operations undertaken during the siege.

These Infernal Spit-fires

By midsummer 1780, the Sultan of Morocco had become noticeably more hostile towards the British, in part because of the payment by Madrid of an annual subsidy of £7,500 in return for leases on the ports of Tetuan and Tangier.[1] Before long, British residents and merchants in Morocco were harassed and the flow of supplies, so useful for the continued resistance by Eliott's garrison, was greatly diminished. 'We may expect no further intercourse with Barbary,' Samuel Ancell wrote to his brother in July:

> The Emperor of Morocco still winks at the hostilities committed by them, and even countenances their illegal proceedings, by permitting the Spanish boats to go out and seize our vessels coming from Tangier ... Several Spanish frigates and xebecs cruising in the Gut, or to the westwards of the Rock.[2]

Don Barcelo's boats enjoyed increasing success, intercepting the blockade-runners trying to get into Gibraltar, and the captured prizes, with colours reversed, were flaunted by their captors before the hungry eyes of the watching garrison. These were mostly British ships, together with Genoan and Venetian craft prepared to run the risk of capture and confiscation in return for the chance of high profits. They were joined, in much smaller numbers than before, by the blockade-runners still coming in across the Straits to land their longed-for cargoes at Europa Point, in defiance of the Sultan's instructions. Captain Drinkwater described the tactics adopted by the Spanish gunboats (which were rather disparagingly referred to, considering the trouble they caused, as bum-boats by the British soldiers and seamen), as they sought to intercept the traffic:

> When the wind was west, two xebecques and four gun-boats anchored at Cabrita Point, cruising at night at the entrance of the bay and in the straits; when easterly, the frigate, xebecques, and

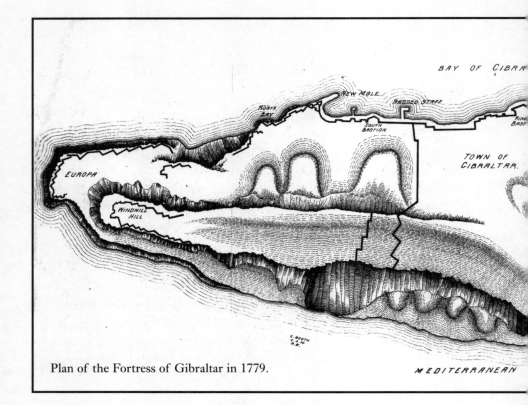

Plan of the Fortress of Gibraltar in 1779.

four gun-boats cruised some between Ceuta and Europa [Point], and others in the Gut; one xebecque was generally observed to lie-to off Europa Point, at the entrance to the bay. Though this disposition apparently obstructed all intercourse between the garrison and our friends in Portugal and Minorca, yet opportunities sometimes occurred when boats shipped out unmolested and returned with the same success.[3]

Bread had become scarce on the Rock, as baking stopped due to a lack of flour, and biscuit, an unappetizing poor substitute, was issued to the soldiers instead: 'Biscuit will be delivered to the regiments in lieu of soft bread from Monday next, the 2d of October, until further orders.'[4] Scurvy, horrible and still little understood, appeared with distressing frequency, and if unchecked, would threaten the ability of the garrison to hold out. This ailment alone was soon disabling considerably more of the garrison than the fire of the Spanish gunners. The exotic remedies tried, which

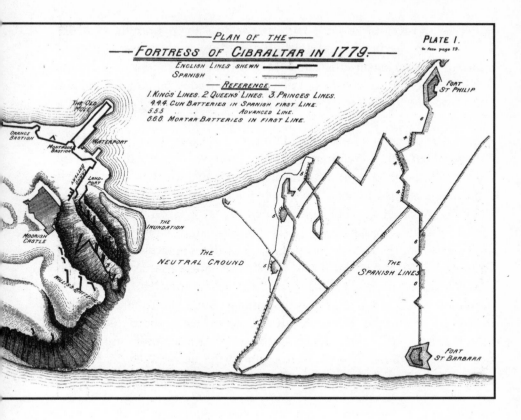

seemed to border on the very edge of quackery, included Acid of Vitriol, Sour Crout (sauerkraut), Extract of Salt and Essence of Spruce, none of which were found to be that effective. John Drinkwater remembered:

> The scurvy made terrible ravages in our hospitals, and more were daily confined: many, however, unwilling to yield to the first attacks, persevered in their duty to the more advanced stages ... The only specific was fresh lemons and oranges, given liberally.'[5]

By good fortune, on 11 October, a Danish Dogger merchantman, outward bound from Malaga as part of a Dutch convoy, was becalmed close to Europa Point. The Gibraltar squadron was out in the Bay, waiting to convoy in two supply ships from Minorca, and the Danish captain was induced to come into harbour by an armed boarding party sent across by Commodore Eliott. The valuable cargo of citrus fruit was immediately purchased by the Governor, and the oranges and lemons issued to those most severely suffering from scurvy. Coming as it did soon after the outbreak of the debilitating disease, this fresh supply of fruit did much to ensure that the hold over the Rock could last. Attempts were made at the same time to seize a Dutch trader, lagging behind the rest of the convoy, but the British boats were driven off by the guns of a vigilant Spanish frigate.

Covert negotiations on a settlement between Great Britain and Spain still rumbled on, sometimes showing promise but usually seeming fruitless. This was due, at least in part, to the tough demands the British representatives had to make to assuage public outrage at any suggestion of giving up the Rock. The talks seemed to play a part in the reluctance of the Spanish commanders to push their campaign against the garrison too hard. From the British viewpoint, it was also a potentially promising strategy to drive a wedge between Madrid and Paris, as the French cannot have been entirely unaware of the discussions, and would have been concerned at possible Spanish duplicity, once Madrid had got what it wanted. Still, the rather languid pace of the operations against Gibraltar changed noticeably in October. Soon after midnight on the first of that month, Spanish troops raided the now rather dilapidated garden allotments in front of the Inundation, spoiling and levelling the meagre crops cultivated there, and setting fire to the palisades at Forbes Barrier, before they were driven off by the picquets. With the dawn it was also seen that a large new battery had begun to be erected under cover of darkness, and the raid was, presumably, intended to cover the noise of the starting of that work.

The Spanish batteries, long in preparation, opened fire on the Rock in earnest, but the gunners were hindered as many of the British positions were sited at such a high elevation that good artillery practice against them was difficult. The handicap could be overcome by the greater use of mortars, and the deployment of these cruelly effective weapons in time came to be a real concern for Eliott. The steadily growing volume of Spanish fire, particularly those guns which proved to have the disconcerting ability to hit targets at ranges of over two miles, indicated clearly the more intense tempo in the operations that had begun. Eliott had the narrow unpaved streets of Gibraltar Town ploughed up into deep furrows, to slow and deflect the round-shot that landed in those alleys, and the efforts to improve and strengthen the more exposed battery positions were redoubled.

The Spanish jabecquillas now completely prevented fishing boats from operating out of the Rock, reducing the food supply for the garrison still further:

> The enemy's gun-boats ... fired on our fishing boats, and obliged them to come in. It is evident their intention is to cut-off the refreshing supply of fish. The ordnance mounted in these boats, discharge 26lb weight and are a great annoyance. They are able to attack ships of force in a calm.[6]

The gunboats also came close inshore each night, to bombard the ships at anchor in Gibraltar harbour, but there was yet another threat to counter. Eliott had a boom constructed from old spars and cables, stretched between the Old Mole and the New Mole, to prevent any Spanish cutting-out parties from getting to the British shipping:

> Finding those nocturnal visits from the gun-boats now so frequent, and knowing it was done with a view to alarm and distress our people, more than with any prospect of reducing the place by such paltry methods, the General came to a resolution to attempt in like manner to rouse and harass their grand camp near the Orange Grove; and for this purpose, whenever their gun-boats made their nightly visits, two double fortified sea-mortars, which had been fixed on the Devil's Tongue, or Old Mole, for the occasion, were constantly fired on the Spanish Camp, and carried their shells into the very centre of it.[7]

While the attention of the garrison was distracted in this way, it was noticed that the forward entrenchments on the isthmus crept steadily onwards, despite the efforts of the gunners in the garrison to slow the work. 'General Alvarez,' Samuel Ancell wrote, 'visits the lines and forts once or twice a week. We know him by his uniform and suite [of staff officers], on which occasion we never fire into the Spanish lines.'[8]

On 12 November 1780, the 200-ton poleacre *Young Sabine*, commanded by Captain McLorg, fought its way past five Spanish xebecs and gunboats, to get into Gibraltar harbour. The *Young Sabine* had a crew of only eighteen seamen, including several young boys, and a light armament, and she came perilously close to being boarded as the Spanish boats swarmed around. Grappling hooks were thrown, and the crews plied their swivel-guns and muskets vigorously, while *Young*

Sabine's sails were torn almost to shreds by Spanish shot. Outward bound from London, McLorg had taken eighteen days to arrive in the Straits, and his safe arrival in harbour, like that of the *Buck* previously, greatly cheered the garrison. He brought in a cargo of cheeses, herrings, rum, smoked hams, flour, sugar, butter and potatoes, all of which were sold for a good price; the captain's gallantry certainly paid a handsome dividend for himself and his crew, for that was the system in place, but was only of use to those who could afford to pay well for the provisions.

Bad weather set in during early December, with heavy rain making life miserable for the troops at both ends of the isthmus, who were every day working in the trenches and gun emplacements with not a dry thread to their backs. So great was the weight of the downpour on one day, that a part of the newly enlarged defences on the Rock were again washed away, as were many of the pathetically small vegetable gardens that the garrison and their families had tried to cultivate in a few fertile patches, to alleviate their meagre and dull diet. The squally weather inevitably slowed the Spanish entrenching work, and at least prevented Don Barcelo's gunboats from putting out into the Bay. Early in 1781 *Young Sabine* worked out of harbour again, nimbly evaded the waiting jabecquillas, and made off to Minorca. McLorg went without one of his crew, however, a French-born man who had stolen a boat and deserted one night to the Spanish lines.

The tedium of the siege was relieved a little early in the New Year, when a deserter from the Spanish lines was arrested on suspicion of being a spy. The man, an NCO, spoke English well, and was noticed to be working upon soldiers of the 58th Foot for information on the state of the defences. Apparently incriminating papers were also found on him, a plan of the defences and a note referring to Europa Point as being a promising and vulnerable place to attack the garrison. Rather strangely, considering the severity of the accusation, the man was not put on trial to answer the charges; he was returned to the Spanish lines under a flag of truce, an undoubtedly lenient course of action. Deserters who came to the Rock subsequently confirmed that he had indeed been spying on the garrison, and was well rewarded for the information he took back.

On 10 January a sorry spectacle appeared at the Ragged Staff Bastion, when two Moroccan galleys approached, unhindered by the watching

Spanish squadron, and landed Mr Logie, the British Consul in Tangier, together with his wife and just over 100 other exhausted, bedraggled and distraught British subjects who had been interned and then expelled by the Sultan. They had been badly treated, manhandled and beaten, their property confiscated, and were hungry and almost in rags. The refugees would probably have starved had the French Consul in Algeciras not provided food for them with money out of his own pocket, before they were sent on to Gibraltar. The malevolent attitude of the Sultan towards what was evidently now presumed to be the doomed British garrison was plain. This was all rather ominous, but five days later, an armed brig sailing out of Madeira brought in seventy butts of fine wine, which must have cheered the garrison a little. News came in on 18 January, with the arrival of the 26-gun cutter *Tartar* (previously a French vessel, taken as a prize by the Royal Navy), bearing a cargo of wine, brandy and olive oil, that Great Britain was now also at war with Holland, and that Dutch shipping should be attacked whenever the opportunity arose. London evidently had few friends at this time, and was rapidly losing those that still remained.

John Drinkwater wrote that observers could see that mortar-boats were being fitted out in Algeciras. These were similar in construction to the rugged gunboats that gave such trouble, but 'The mortars were fixed in a solid bed of timber, in the centre of the boat; and the only apparent distinction was that they had long prows and braced their yards more athwart the boat when they fired.'[9] The operations of the mortar-boats became another headache for Eliott just like the more numerous jabecqillas. French naval commanders were aware that a tight blockade in the difficult currents of the Straits would always be imperfect, especially given the high profits that the swift Barbary blockade-runners and other privateers could make from a successful cruise. The almost daily blockade-running in to the Rock, although hazardous, often intercepted by Don Barcelo's squadron, and not of itself sufficient to sustain the garrison, could not be shut down completely. Spanish experience so far showed that this was so, and Rodney had seemed to sweep the high seas clear of opposition as his great supply convoy approached the Rock. They had a distinct preference for maintaining a combined fleet in the English Channel and the Western Approaches, stifling any attempt at another major resupply effort, before the slow-moving transports could even be assembled for convoy by Royal Navy warships. Elsewhere in the Mediterranean, French activity was quickening. On 19 February Samuel Ancell recalled, 'This afternoon a brig arrived from Minorca in four and a half days, with wine, sugar and brandy. Two xebecs in vain, stretched across but could not get near her, the wind blowing very strong. She brings the intelligence that the French have blockaded Minorca.'[10] News was also received that the frigate HMS *Brilliant*, commanded by Captain Robert Curtis and intending to come into Gibraltar harbour, had been chased through the straits at night by Spanish warships, but had made her way safely to Minorca.

Long months of siege had passed, with brief spurts of danger and excitement, but the chances to display valour and gain advancement were few. Officers fretted at the lack of opportunity to shine, and obtain preferment and promotion. John Drinkwater recalled:

> They could not help feeling the peculiar hardship of their situation; nor was the inactive and tedious service of a blockaded garrison at all calculated to divert their minds, or to soothe them into an acquiescence with their fortune. They reflected, with no very agreeable sensations, upon the preferment which had been liberally bestowed upon young officers in England, while many subalterns in Gibraltar had ten or twelve years of strict duty and service to plead.[11]

In addition to sickness and the tedium of dull routine, real hardship, if not actual starvation, was being felt by the whole garrison; bags of stale breadcrumbs were selling at a shilling a pound. 'A very little time', Eliott wrote to Major General James Murray, the commander of the garrison in Minorca, 'will reduce us to the utmost straits.'[12] Although the Governor had early in the siege given orders that all supplies, other than those of the official ration scale, should be sold openly in public and not brought in to the Rock by private arrangements, those ordinary soldiers who had little or no money to purchase a few comforts and extras suffered particularly badly, as did their unfortunate families. The official rations often seemed inadequate, and Mrs Catherine Upton, an officer's wife with little enough to spare, wrote of one wretched woman, 'She sat weeping at my door with two children', attempting to suckle her baby while her other child, a young boy, begged her to give him some bread.[13]

The Spanish gunboats were becoming more bold in their attacks: 'A woman was cut in two as she was drawing on her stockings. These infernal spit-fires can attack any quarter of the Garrison as they please,' wrote Kate Upton with some bitterness.[14] The blockade, an expedient policy while the French and Spanish pursued campaigns elsewhere, had taken some time to bite, but had now begun to threaten Eliott's ability to hold out. Poor diet, boredom and sickness took a noticeable toll on morale and manpower alike. Supplies for the garrison were running low, despite the enterprising blockade-runners, and Eliott wrote in a despondent tone to Murray in Minorca:

> I fear 'tis reasonable to apprehend (however determined the intentions may be at home) that no convoy from Great Britain can with certainty be depended on, considering the various and important service our fleet must be called upon to perform in opposition to such armaments as threaten from every quarter ...
> If you will be pleased to spare as much of your provisions in store as may be done with safety to the island.[15]

As yet unknown to Eliott and his garrison, Vice Admiral George Darby sailed from Spithead on 13 March 1781 on board HMS *Britannia* (100). The Admiral gathered his convoy together off Cork, comprising ships destined for the West Indies and the Indian Ocean, as well as for the resupply of Gibraltar and Minorca. Meeting no interference on the way, Darby appeared off Cape Spartel on the North African coast on 11 April, with twenty-one ships-of-the-line, ten frigates, four fire-ships, and ninety-seven heavily laden merchantmen under escort. Over twelve anxious months had passed since the first relief by Rodney, and the soldiers' rations had been progressively reduced, less than a pound of bread or biscuit a day for each man, and a pound of beef each week (often rancid – 'quite rotten and stinking' according to Miriam Green).[16] Morale and discipline in the garrison suffered accordingly, and on 28 March two soldiers of the 56th Foot were hanged for robbery. Three young officers of the 72nd Foot were also fined severely for threatening merchants who had provided them with stores and were pressing, not unreasonably, for payment.

Alliance warfare is never simple, and the French and Spanish naval commanders had made a poor job of trying to intercept Darby's ships. Commodore La Motte-Picquet, in Brest, missed the chance to catch the fleet and merchantmen on the way south, and then failed to combine his forces with Admiral de Cordoba in Cadiz. La Motte-Picquet urged his Spanish counterpart to come north, while de Cordoba hoped that the French squadron would come to Cadiz. The confusion and delay that resulted gave Darby unhindered passage, a gift he could scarcely have hoped for. Had the two commanders managed to work together effectively, Darby could hardly have fought his way through to the Rock, encumbered with the slow-moving transports, for de Cordoba alone had thirty ships-of-the-line under command. La Motte-Picquet did capture a British convoy to the west of the Scilly Isles, bringing twenty-two merchantmen into Brest as prizes, heavily laden with cargoes valued at five million pounds sterling. However, the French Ambassador in Madrid was far from optimistic over the chances for the Spanish Navy on its own being able to prevent Darby's resupply operation. Despite having well-founded warships in good numbers, a fearful repeat of the destruction of de Langara's squadron was predicted:

> The Spanish fleet returned to Cadiz ... I am not at all anxious that it should meet with the British and am much relieved to know that it is in safety. In the present circumstances a defeat would have the most disastrous consequences in every way. I was quite aware that there is no glory in entering harbour when the enemy approaches, but at any rate there remains thirty battleships in fairly good condition ... The King should preserve his fleet so as to cover the seas and guard the coasts, protect trade to the Indies.[17]

So, tempted by what might be achieved, but burdened with concern at what might befall them, the Spanish naval commanders took no very active steps to halt Darby and his convoy – it seemed clear that the sharp memory of the calamitous 'Moonlight Battle' in the early weeks of 1780 lingered on. This failure of nerve had enormous consequences, for, had Darby been engaged on the high seas and been defeated or even just turned back, Gibraltar must have been lost through starvation and Minorca would have fallen soon after.

Once darkness fell on the evening of 4 April, four longboats crowded with armed soldiers and seamen set out from the New Mole to try to cut out a Spanish sloop and two fire-ships anchored off Cabrita Point. It had been hoped that the cloudy night would cover the attempt, but the sky cleared, and the boats were fired on by batteries on the shore, and had to withdraw with some haste. The following day the *Eagle*, a privateer sailing out of Glasgow, made her way into harbour, slipping past the prowling gunboats with word that another convoy was drawing near. The Royal Navy cutter HMS *Kite*, commanded by Captain Trollop, arrived in the Bay four days later with the welcome confirmation that Darby's fleet, with a large number of merchantmen crammed with valuable stores of every kind, would arrive the very next day.

The transports began to come into Gibraltar harbour at daybreak. Their close escorts easily brushed aside the gunboats that tried rather lamely to interrupt their progress. John Drinkwater remembered:

> At daybreak, on the 12th April, the much expected fleet under the command of Admiral Darby, was in sight from our signal stations ... The fog gradually rose, like the curtain of a vast theatre, discovering to the anxious garrison ... one of the most beautiful and pleasing scenes it is possible to conceive. The convoy, consisting of near a hundred vessels, was in a compact body, while the majority of the line of battle-ships lay-to under the Barbary shore, having orders not to enter the Bay, lest the enemy should molest them with their fire-ships.[18]

The Spaniards gave up the attempt to prevent the ships from entering the Bay, and withdrew in such haste before the advancing fleet that several of their gunboats ran aground, and were abandoned by their crews. By some oversight and perhaps in the excitement of the convoy's arrival, nothing was done to destroy them before they could be recovered. 'The whole town was elated, viewing the glorious sight of this great fleet entering the port, the morning pleasantly delightful, and the men-of-war and merchant vessels, amounting together to near 100 sail, stretched all along the Barbary coast.'[19]

By mid-morning the leading ships had come to anchor and troops detailed for the task began unloading the supplies. Shortly before midday they were bombarded by the Spanish gunners; battery after battery joined in, and soon 114 large guns and mortars, in addition to fifteen gunboats, were firing at the supply ships. The unloading of the cargoes had to be moved to the relatively sheltered New Mole, but even so the longer-range Spanish fire remained troublesome. 'Their shells fell short, one only struck the side of the *Nottingham*, East Indiaman, and the fuse

breaking off it fell into the water.'[20] Rear Admiral Sir John Ross supervised the unloading of the transports, and hundreds of seamen were
detailed to assist in the work, to speed matters along. Frustrated of
success against the transports, the Spanish gunners then directed their
fire at Gibraltar Old Town, parts of which were soon well alight. 'A call
to arms prevents my further writing,' Samuel Ancell noted in his journal:

> The enemy have opened all their batteries on the town, confusion
> and consternation are everywhere to be seen ... From Waterport
> to Southport houses are blazing and shot battering those that will
> not burn ... One minute a shot batters a house about your ears,
> and the next a shell drops at your feet.[21]

The poor inhabitants of the town, who had been celebrating the safe
arrival of the convoy with its promise of plenty, were forced to flee to the
southern end of the Rock once more. One of their number, a priest
named Father Mesa, had the presence of mind to rescue the venerated
statue of the Virgin Mary, 'Our Lady of Europe', from the chapel shrine
in which it was kept, and took it to safety before it could be consumed by
the flames.

Some of those of the garrison who were at liberty to do so, braved the
bombardment to see what loot was to be found in the abandoned and
battered houses. Most of the soldiers had been on short and unappetizing
rations for some time, and they were indignant to find some storerooms
bulging with stocks of hoarded food and luxuries. John Drinkwater
recalled:

> The extreme distress to which the soldiers had been reduced by
> the venary conduct of the hucksters and liquor-dealers, in
> hoarding, or rather concealing the stocks, to enhance the price of
> what was exposed for sale, raised amongst the troops ... a spirit
> of revenge.[22]

Drink in large quantities was certainly discovered, and drunken
soldiers soon became an unruly mob, undeterred by the flying shot and
shell, the razor-sharp iron splinters and jagged broken fragments of
masonry thick in the air. 'Their discipline was over-powered by their
inebriation, and from that instant, regardless of punishment or the
entreaties of their officers, they were guilty of many and great
excesses.' Drinkwater went on to say, 'Any soldier convicted of being

General Sir George Augustus Eliott, the Defender of Gibraltar, holding the keys of the Rock in his hands.

Lieutenant General Robert Boyd, Deputy Governor of Gibraltar.

Captain Roger Curtis, RN. His gunboats fought for control of Gibraltar Bay.

Admiral George Brydges Rodney, victor of the Moonlight Battle, who brought the first relief convoy to Gibraltar.

King Carlos III of Spain, whose ambitions for the recovery of Gibraltar took Spain to war with Great Britain in 1779.

The Rock from Fort St Barbara, on the Spanish Lines. A late 19th century photograph.

Gibraltar under siege, viewed from the Queen of Spain's Chair.

Gibraltar at the time of the Great Siege, viewed from the Gut.

The old Land-Port defences. A late 19th century photograph.

Lieutenant Koehler's depress gun-carriage.

The Great Sortie, 27 November 1781. Eliott and his staff officers watch the operation at close quarters.

The battering ships' attack, drawn by Lieutenant Sandby, 12th Foot, an eye-witness.

A Spanish floating battery. Guns only mounted on the port side.

The battering ships' attack, 13 September 1782.

The battering ships' attack, 13–14 September 1782. Captain Curtis's rescue attempt.

The *San Domingo* blowing up during the Moonlight Battle, 16 January 1780.

The arrival of Howe's relief convoy, October 1782, before the Battle of Cape Spartel.

drunk or asleep at his post, or found marauding, should be immediately executed.' Some looters, however, having found stocks of drink, defied the patrols sent to restore order and barricaded themselves into the buildings, refusing to stagger out until they had drunk their fill. Not all the soldiers in the town forgot their duty, though, and the Governor wrote afterwards that the Hanoverian troops had no part in the shocking outbreak of indiscipline.

Kate Upton remembered huddling against a wall with her two small children, Charlotte and Jack, as the bombardment went on: 'A ball struck the rock against which I leaned and covered us with dust and stones ... In a few minutes after, a shell burst so near us, I had scarcely time to run out of the way.'[23] A soldier of the 58th Foot showed her where to find shelter in Montague's Bastion, and sent her on her way with the encouraging words, 'Never fear, Madam, if the damn'd Dons fire to eternity they will never take the old rock.' The firing ceased in the early afternoon, as the Spanish gunners took their customary rest, but began again with fresh fury at about 5pm, and continued to be directed at the vengeful but militarily insignificant task of demolishing the town. 'The enemy keep up a vigorous bombardment upon us,' Samuel Ancell wrote, 'The town is almost become a heap of ruins, and what few houses are left standing, the walls are so shattered, that it is not safe to go in them.'[24] Ancell came across a private from his own regiment in the street, quite plainly drunk, waving a bottle, and oblivious of the danger from the Spanish fire. 'Damn me,' the man called out, 'if I don't like fighting. Plenty of good liquor for carrying away, never was the price so cheap.' At that instant a flying shell fragment shattered the bottle in the man's hand as he offered it to Ancell to take a pull. 'That is not any loss,' he muttered with a shrug and a conspiratorial wink, 'I have found a whole cask.'[25]

For a time, British counter-battery fire concentrated on the San Carlos Battery, which was silenced temporarily, but the Spanish gunners maintained their efforts in the following days, trying to halt the unloading of stores and supplies. Eliott asked Darby to land most of the stocks of gunpowder held in the magazines of his warships, to augment the supplies of the garrison, not knowing when, and if, the next convoy would make its way through. The Admiral promptly agreed – although he might have to fight his way back out into the Atlantic, the recent performance of the Spanish naval commanders seemed to make this event unlikely. Normal rations for those on the Rock were restored now that the storehouses had been replenished, and the Daily Orders for the garrison ran: 'Full allowance of Beef and Pork, five ounces of Butter, quarter of a pint of Oil, one pint Pease, ditto Kidney Beans, two pints of Wheat, twelve ounces of Raisins, to be served tomorrow.'[26]

On 18 April a brisk little battle was fought in the Bay when Spanish xebecs moved in and attacked the frigates *Minerva*, *Monsieur* and *Nonsuch*, inflicting casualties but no serious damage, before they were driven off. A similar attempt the next day was also unsuccessful, although Darby wrote of the difficulty in countering their nimble tactics: 'The gun-boats in calm operated against our frigates by means of their oars and were secure from pursuit.'[27] It was rumoured that the quality of the Spanish gunpowder had improved to such a degree that they could lay off the anchorage at a range that prevented the Royal Navy ships, or the land batteries, from replying with real effect. The Admiral denied this, assuring Their Lordships in the Admiralty in London that it was the great barrel-length of the large guns mounted in the bows of the gunboats that gave them a superior range against the shorter British pieces.

Two days later, on the evening of 20 April, Darby made use of a north-easterly breeze and sailed with his warships and the accompanying merchantmen. None of the Tyne colliers that had come in with the convoy could be unloaded in the time available, so these were beached beside the New Mole, so that their cargoes could be taken off as needed. Darby got away from the Bay without serious interference, apart from a few parting shots from the Spanish gunboats. Samuel Ancell wrote rather wistfully, 'In the evening they were all out of sight. The Spanish towers, as usual, spread the alarm.'[28] The Admiral took with him dispatches and letters from Eliott to London, and about 1,000 sick, wounded and fugitive civilians, further reducing the demands on the food supplies in Gibraltar. He evaded the French cruising squadrons, and got safely back to the Lizard Point in Cornwall just over three weeks later, at the close of a fine naval operation of high importance, carried off with remarkably little loss.

This second relief convoy saved the garrison in Gibraltar from starvation once again. Lesser resupply operations continued, and on 27 April a flotilla of sixteen small ships and three privateers all laden with provisions from Minorca were convoyed safely into harbour, under escort of HMS *Enterprise*, the frigates *Brilliant*, *Porcupine* and *Minorca*, and the sloop *Fortune*. They also brought in two Spanish xebecs that had been overhauled in the fresh breeze of the Gut and forced to submit. Don Barcelo had begun to prepare his ships to put to sea as the small convoy approached, but then appears to have changed his mind, and stayed in harbour, leaving the xebecs to fend for themselves.

On 28 April, *Enterprise* and *Minorca* sailed for England, escorting several merchantmen, and once again, apart from firing signal rockets along the coast, the Spanish did not attempt to interfere. It became clear that their siege operation had now become a rather limping affair, and the Rock would not be starved out while the Royal Navy could operate so effectively in this way. Still, on the wider strategic stage, the very necessary employment of Darby's fleet to convoy the supply ships safely in to sustain Gibraltar allowed the French Admiral Pierre-André de Suffren to set out from Brest unobserved and unmolested – he took his own squadron to the Indian Ocean, where he did a good deal of damage to British shipping and interests. Not only that. Admiral de Grasse had also taken advantage of the distraction to sail his fleet to the West Indies and the Atlantic seaboard of America, in a move that eventually would prove fatal to General Cornwallis and the British Army at Yorktown in Virginia that October. Darby's success in resupplying the Rock, an undoubtedly fine achievement, had been bought at a high strategic price.

Eliott continued to look for ways to combat the activities of the Spanish gunboats, and two supply ships that had been unable to leave with Darby were cut down and each equipped with eight guns. These makeshift gunboats, named *Vanguard* and *Repulse*, were moored at the end of the Old Mole, and their weight of fire was a useful addition to that of the land batteries nearby. Improvements also had to be made to the defences, which were deteriorating as the daily bombardment went on:

> Our batteries, especially at Willis's, by this time exhibited a very
> disorderly and ruinous appearance … The lines were also nearly
> choked up with loose stones and rubbish; brought down by the
> shot from the rock above; the traverses along the line-wall were
> greatly injured, and the town, particularly at the north end,

approached every day toward complete destruction.[29]

Stern measures had been imposed to restore discipline among the garrison after recent disorder. Examples had to be made, and on 4 May the Order of the Day read:

> The criminal, John Wild of the 58th Regiment, to be executed at guard mounting tomorrow at the storehouse where he committed the robbery, with a label on which is to be wrote the word PLUNDERER, the body to remain hanging until sunset ... All the 58th Regiment not on duty to attend the execution.[30]

Eliott wrote to the commander-in-chief, Lord Amherst, on 17 May 1781, with a rueful account of the disorders among the troops since Darby's relief:

> I must not conceal from you the scandalous irregularity of the British regiments comprising the garrison ever since the enemy opened their Batteries; except the Rapes and Murders, there is no one crime but what they have been repeatedly guilty of and that in the most daring manner; altho' many have been tried and convicted before General Courts Martial of the most heinous offences yet only one has been condemned to death [presumably this was Wild of the 58th] ... Things are so bad that not a sentinel at his post but will connive at and assist in robbing over the King's Stores under his charge ... I must declare that the Hanoverians have committed no public outrage and I believe but few private, having maintained apparent good order despite of the most dissolute examples.[31]

The Governor also found that he had to urge his artillery officers to exercise restraint in their handling of the gunboat attacks. Although Darby's relief had been timely and welcome, there was no telling when, or indeed if, another major convoy would get through to the Rock. Good husbanding of supplies and ammunition was always necessary. Spanish gun and mortar-boats had approached and fired from a fair distance at the New Mole and the town; the bombardment, little more than nuisance fire, had gone on for about an hour when the exasperated British gunners opened a heavy cannonade to drive the Spanish vessels away. In doing so, some 400 round-shot were fired off, all of which went into the deep waters of the Bay, as no hits seem to have been obtained. 'There would be no end of expending ammunition,' Eliott wrote rather tartly, 'if we fired every time they came, and while they were at so great a distance ... In future no notice [is] to be taken of the gunboats until they have approached within the distance of grape.'[32]

The wearisome Spanish bombardment went on, fierce and noisy enough, and certainly damaging to the now rather pathetic Old Town, but inflicting little lasting harm on the defences. The Rock Gun, high up on the North Face, had become a favoured target, with frequent casualties among the gunners serving there. In the midst of the steady daily trickle of injuries sustained, it was remembered that one particularly unfortunate soldier 'was in the office [privy] easing Nature when a Ball took off his head and left his Body, the only remains to finishing Nature's cause.'[33]

Samuel Ancell wrote to his brother on 20 May of an enterprising, but remarkably inept, attempt by a Spanish officer to scout the defences on the Rock:

> Last night a man was discovered in slow steps towards the garrison, on the road leading from Bay-side to Landport; but when he came pretty near the advanced guard, he crawled upon his hands and knees; a Hanoverian serjeant, on duty there, challenged him before he came as far as the works, upon which he made a retreat ... A gold-laced hat was picked up on the road, which makes us imagine that he was an officer in the enemy's service.[34]

In the wider war, far away from the narrow confines of the Rock and the Straits of Gibraltar, a League of Armed Neutrality had been formed by Denmark, Russia and Sweden, to resist the enforced searches of their vessels and the confiscation of cargoes by the cruising squadrons of the Royal Navy. Spanish diplomatic activity had played a role in this agreement, and Madrid was pleased with the result:

> We also induced the Empress of Russia [Catherine II] to place herself at the head of almost all the Neutral Nations to support the honour of her flag ... Thus was England deprived of the resources she might have drawn from the maritime Powers, not excepting even Holland, her ancient ally.[35]

The League of Armed Neutrality could claim to maintain over eighty ships-of-the-line at sea, considerably more than the Royal Navy could muster, with its concurrent multiple commitments on both sides of the Atlantic, in the Mediterranean supporting both Gibraltar and Minorca, and the Indian Ocean. Great Britain, at open war with France, Spain and Holland and many of her American colonists, had not often been so devoid of close friends. However, an agreement had been reached by the Admiralty to obtain supplies of pine timber (for masts) from Denmark to satisfy the hungry requirements of the Royal Navy's Dockyards, and Russia soon regretted the loss of the revenue from these valuable exports. This trade was resumed as before, and in a curious way, the effective neutralization of the Baltic and northern waters relieved the British of having to make any effort to protect their shipping in those regions. Spain's diplomatic success with the League was, therefore, nowhere near as clear as it at first seemed.

This Glorious Occasion

Spanish troops strengthened their forward batteries on the level ground of the isthmus during June 1781, adding to the long-established formal works between Fort St Philip and Fort St Barbara. Four new large batteries were constructed – the Black, Infanta, Prince's, and Princess's, with a total of forty-nine heavy pieces of artillery. There were now also in place a number of powerful mortars in the intervening lines and at the San Carlos battery, whose elevation had the valuable ability to reach the highest British batteries on the Rock. Six of the siege guns were also set at an unusually high angle, the trails being dug into pits – known to the Spanish as being *d'empotada*, to increase their range.

Samuel Ancell recalled that an accident in the Spanish lines helped to relieve the tedium: 'A magazine belonging to the enemy on the rising ground under the Queen's Chair took fire … There was a great explosion, and it is computed near five thousand shells were destroyed, besides many lives lost.'[1] The dull routine of garrison life was also briefly lifted on 7 July 1781 when the sloop *Helena*, inward bound for the Rock, was seen to be becalmed on a glassy smooth sea at the entrance to the Bay. The commander, Captain Roberts, had the sweeps out and the crew were pulling lustily for the shelter of the harbour, but Spanish jabecqillas were moving swiftly from their station off Algeciras to intercept his course. A fresh westerly breeze blew up, and *Vanguard* and *Repulse* put out into the Bay to support the small vessel. Despite heavy shot splintering the fragile scantlings of the sloop, Roberts was able to bring *Helena* into safety with the astonishingly small loss of just one man killed (the boatswain) and two others lightly wounded, although almost all her sails and rigging were shot to shreds. A boat bearing a flag of truce put out from Algeciras soon afterwards and approached the Rock, with a Spanish officer who called out to enquire why the garrison had been firing on neutral ships. Eliott's dry and uncompromising response to the rather irrelevant question was that they should stay out of range in future.

The dreariness and squalor of closely confined garrison life, even when under bombardment, was occasionally relieved by the social niceties, and the wives in the garrison did their best, in very reduced circumstances, to maintain a home life for husbands and families. It was of course by no means only the soldiers and seamen who were under the daily lash of the Spanish gunners, and Miriam Green recalled that 'a very Good Young Woman, and a child of three months, were blown out of the tent by a shell ... They were thrown into a deep gulley, and the child tore to pieces, and the Woman much burnt and otherwise wounded.'[2] Those who had the means arranged small supper parties, and in the fine weather picnics of a spartan kind were held on the less exposed slopes at the southern end of the Rock. Rations were once again meagre and monotonous, and Samuel Ancell wrote that a Portuguese blockade-runner, laden with cattle, had been taken into Algeciras by the Spanish cruisers: 'This will be a great loss to the garrison, as we have not received a supply of fresh meat for some time ... The fresh provision, which is sold now, is pork, and that is very indifferent and scarce, fed on the filth of the place.'[3]

There was certainly a kind of grim siege humour to be had also. An enterprising soldier with an eye for loot found a haul of silver pocket-watches and other jewellery in the ruins of one of the houses in the town. Knowing that he would be unable to take his booty back into a crowded barrack-room and keep it safe, he pushed the haul, wrapped up tightly in a cloth, into the muzzle of a 24-pounder gun in one of the quieter batteries, hoping to recover the looted goods later. However, as luck would have it, the piece was discharged at one of the prowling jabecquillas the very next day, silver watches, trinkets and all. The puzzlement of the Spanish seamen at being subjected to this particular form of curiously valuable langridge-shot may well be imagined.

Sharp criticism was directed at some of the medical staff for shirking their duty under fire. Several of the regimental surgeons and their assistants were found to be very reluctant to leave their bomb-proof shelters until the regular periods of bombardment ceased. Inadequate supplies of field dressings and bandages had been provided to the battery positions, and the wounded had to lie and suffer in the open, tended and made comfortable, after a rudimentary fashion, by their comrades, but without medical attention. As a result the casualties sometimes bled to death before receiving proper treatment. John Drinkwater remembered:

> Our casualties consequently began again to be pretty frequent amongst our parties ... A soldier of the 72nd lost his leg by a shot from Fort St Barbara. He bore amputation with prodigious firmness, but died soon afterwards through the loss of blood, previous to his being brought to the hospital. This fact being represented to the Governor, the sergeants of the different regiments were ordered to attend the hospital to be taught by the surgeons how to apply the tourniquets; which was afterwards productive of very beneficial consequences. Tourniquets were also distributed to the different guards, to be at hand in case of necessity.

The Captain went on to recall, 'A shell fell into a house in the town, in which Ensign Stephens of the 39th was sitting; imagining himself not safe where he was, he quitted the room to get to a more secure place, but just as he passed the door the shell burst, and a splinter mortally wounded him.'[4]

A sign of declining morale and discipline on the Rock was shown by an attempted mutiny by crewman on the naval cutter *Speedwell*. The discovered plot was to overpower their officer and sail the cutter to Algeciras, and once there to sell the vessel to the Spanish authorities for a handsome price. The ringleaders were put in irons, and could have expected the most draconian punishment; surprisingly, they were instead released and allowed to return to duty. Despite the seriousness of the intended offence, a degree of leniency was applied, and it seemed that it was understood what the dull routine of endless days in a siege town, with little diversion other than strong drink, could do to the judgement of otherwise reliable men. Great attention was, however, devoted to the various means by which the gunners sought to improve their techniques, and so add to the burden of the besieging troops. 'Quadrants, spirit-levels and instruments of various forms and machinery adorn the batteries,' Samuel Ancell rather facetiously recalled, 'for the most exact and certain method of killing. I suppose in a few weeks more practice, they will be so expert in levelling a gun that should a Spaniard raise his head above the epaulment, it will be immediately severed from his shoulders.'[5]

The work of the Spanish batteries lessened in intensity for the time being, and by the end of the summer, some days saw only three token shots fired at the garrison, referred to rather irreverently by the soldiers as the Trinity. Two young lads proved particularly adept at spotting incoming shells and round-shot, and giving early warning to their comrades to take cover. They earned the amusingly tolerant nicknames 'Shot' and 'Shell' from the soldiers. Such a very languid bombardment as the Spanish now made was plainly not going to drive Eliott and his men from the Rock, although the besiegers did have their occasional successes, and the activity had apparently become a holding operation while the British garrison in Minorca were under attack. Samuel Ancell wrote:

> The enemy continue their long-range shells upon the Southward which is a great annoyance. Last night a shell fell under the platform of a tent where two corporals were asleep ... The shell lay burning under the boards, when they opened the tent door to let in the air, to prevent being suffocated, at that instant it exploded, and blew them some yards, without receiving any injury, they shortly recovered from their surprise and turned their eyes to the place where the tent had stood ... We learn that the French have landed an army on Minorca.[6]

On the evening of 19 September 1781 a shot fired from the Spanish lines hit the Town-Major's house, collapsing a wall onto that officer, and two others of the 39th Foot. Major Burke's leg was badly broken in the blast, an injury that proved fatal. 'When assistance came,' John Drinkwater remembered,

> they found Major Burke almost buried amongst the ruins of the room. He was instantly conveyed to the hospital, where he soon died after the wounded part was amputated, much lamented by his friends ... Majors Mercier and Vignoles had time to escape before the shell burst; they were nevertheless slightly wounded by the shell splinters, as were a sergeant of the 39th, and his daughter, who were in the cellar underneath ... Captain Fowlis of the 73rd was appointed town-major.[7]

Such a daily toll of casualties, each incident in itself small enough, imperceptibly but certainly drained the strength of the garrison and their families, in just such a way as the drab, monotonous diet sapped the health, and the dullness of routine and anguish at lack of opportunity lowered their spirit and sense of discipline.

The approach trenches snaked steadily across the isthmus, coming ever nearer to the Rock, and more powerful Spanish batteries of guns and mortars were in place and brought into action. 'A person would think it impossible for a bird to escape amidst the showers of shot,' according to Miriam Green.[8] On 22 October, the British gunners made a special effort to demolish a newly constructed battery opposite the Water-Port Gate, but the attempt had to be abandoned after more than 2,000 round-shot and explosive shells had been fired, without achieving very much damage. In time, the whole water frontage from the Old Mole to the New Mole, and even further to the south, would come under fire; when that happened, the unloading of shipping would become impossible and the garrison would eventually starve. It seemed plain that, at some point, an infantry sortie would have to be made across the Neutral Ground to put a stop to the besiegers entrenching themselves so close to the Rock. Eliott watched the daily progress of the Spanish workmen, and took the bold decision to strike first, and ruin both the newly constructed artillery emplacements and any, as yet unseen, preparations being made for an attempt to storm the defences.

Two Walloon deserters came over to the garrison on 21 November and were closely questioned by the Governor; neither had any hesitation in describing the extent and layout of the forward works, and pointing out their various features. They added that some 21,000 Spanish troops were now in the besieging lines and adjacent camps. The obvious risk in attempting any sortie against such a substantial force was that the depleted garrison, where scurvy was still a problem, might incur irreplaceable casualties in the assault. Still, the chance of spoiling the recently constructed Spanish works was sufficient for the Governor to act, despite the risk. It had been noted that the newly constructed lines had no flanking protection, and batteries were not sited to fire across the front of the lines and take any attackers in enfilade. So, any Spanish fire from the depth batteries and trenches closer to San Roques would be largely masked by the presence of their own forward lines.

The plan that Eliott prepared for the sortie on the night of 26–27 November 1781 was quite straightforward – under cover of darkness, three attacking columns would skirt the Inundation obstacle, cross the 800 yards or so from the North Face of the Rock, storm the forward

Spanish entrenchments, level them, burn the stores and spike the guns and mortars. Simple enough, but such operations in the dark hours were fraught with difficulty, with the essential level of command and control made more demanding, and the added risk of confusion as to who was friend and who was foe. If the Spanish sentries were alert, and gave the alarm soon enough, there would be heavy fighting and losses that could not be made good. Nonetheless, Eliott made his arrangements; a soldier from the 58th Foot made the journey across the sands and deserted, but no hint of the impending operation became known, and the man took little information of real value with him. The first most in the garrison knew of what was intended was when the wine-shops in the town were closed at 6pm that day, earlier than usual, and troops detailed to fall with their arms and accoutrements, ready for the forthcoming task.

The whole operation was under the command of Brigadier General Charles Ross, now restored to favour after his absurd feud with Robert Boyd. The Evening Orders for the garrison ran:

> All the grenadiers and light infantry of the garrison, and all the men of the 12th and Hardenberg's Regiments, and non-commissioned officers now on duty, to be immediately relieved, and to join their regiments, to form a detachment consisting of the 12th and Hardenberg's Regiments complete, the grenadiers and light infantry of the other regiments (which are to be completed to their full establishments from the battalion companies), one captain, three lieutenants, ten non-commissioned officers, and 100 artillery[men], and three engineers, seven officers, and twelve non-commissioned officers, overseers, with 146 workmen from the line, and forty from the artificer company. Each man to have thirty-six rounds of ammunition, with a good flint in his piece, and another in his pocket. No drums to go out, except two with each regiment. No volunteers will be allowed. The whole to be commanded by Brigadier-General Ross; and to assemble on the Red Sands at twelve o'clock tonight, to make a sortie upon the enemy's batteries. The 39th and 58th Regiments to parade under the command of Brigadier-General Picton, to sustain the sortie if necessary. Counter-sign 'Steady'.[9]

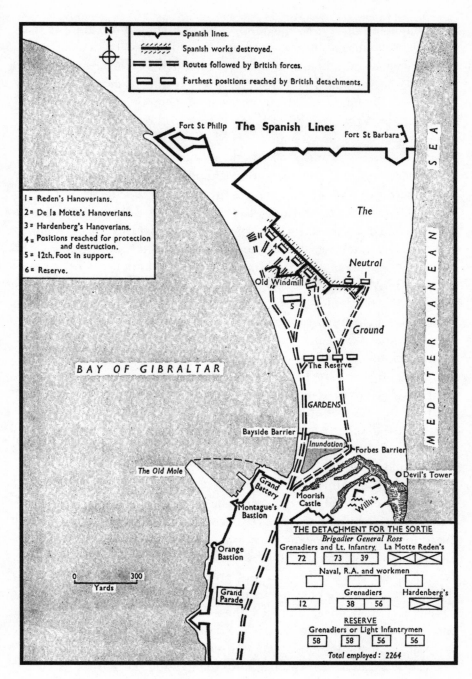

The Great Sortie, 27 November 1781.

The comment that 'No volunteers will be allowed' did not indicate that enthusiasm on the part of otherwise under-employed soldiers to take part in an audacious raid should be discouraged. 'Such was the general ardour to partake in the bold Enterprise that every man considered himself as unfortunate, who was obliged to remain behind.'[10] Under Eliott's watchful eye, Ross gave his detailed orders to the commanders of the three attacking columns, and by 7pm, the quartermasters had begun issuing the necessary picks, staves and axes to those men detailed to act as pioneers, while the engineers were equipped with slow matches, flints and tinderboxes with which to create ruin in the Spanish lines.

The left-hand column, under the command of Lieutenant Colonel Trigge, comprised the 12th Foot, the Light Company of the 58th Foot, and the Light and Grenadier Companies of the 72nd Foot, together with some artillerymen, and 100 seamen under Captain Curtis and Lieutenants Muckle and Campbell, RN, to act as pioneers in the work of destruction. This column comprised some 824 men in all. Lieutenant Colonel Dachenhausen commanded the centre column – 620 men from the Light and Grenadier Companies of the 39th Foot, the Grenadier Companies of the 56th and 58th Foot, and the Light and Grenadier Companies of the 73rd Foot, together with gunners and pioneers. The right-hand column, composed mostly of Hanoverian troops, was commanded by Lieutenant Colonel Hugo, with the Grenadier Companies of Reden's Regiment and De la Motte's Regiment, the Light Company of the 56th Foot, and Hardenberg's Regiment, together with gunners and pioneers, 570 men in total. The force that was devoted to the sortie was 2,014 strong, a very substantial part of the fittest men in the garrison, as only 2,431 troops would be left to go on guard, excluding those lying sick in hospital. The risk was great if things went wrong, and the continued security of the Rock was at stake, but the promised reward for success was substantial. Eliott was not content to cautiously sit behind stout defences and await events, but proved this night that he was very able and ready to take risks for an appropriately promising return.

Hugo's right-hand column led the attack, moving through Forbes Barrier shortly before 3am on 27 November. The attacking troops filed out past the marshy Inundation, and set off smartly into the darkness. The centre column went through both the Bayside and Forbes Barriers, with the left column under Trigge bringing up the rear. Despite the unavoidable noise in getting thousands of armed men with all their accoutrements and equipment through the barriers in the darkness, the important element of surprise was almost complete – the moon had set, which no doubt helped, although British and Hanoverian troops on the right fired at each other in the gloom at one point. The Spanish sentries were soon alerted, but they may have believed that the movement across the Neutral Ground was that of deserters coming in from the garrison. Precious moments were lost, and they were only able to get off a few shots before falling back in haste. A few men gamely stood their ground, and in the centre column, Lieutenant Dacres of the 39th Foot narrowly escaped injury when a Spanish soldier fired his musket into his face at close range, but missed his shot in the poor light. On the right, Colonel Hugo called to his men to form line and hurry forward to the entrenchments, which were found to be almost completely unoccupied, and the soldiers immediately began to level the positions with shovels and hatchets, knock over the casks and gabions filled with sand and stones, and fill in the defensive ditch.

The forward Spanish lines had clearly been held by only a scratch night-watch, and troops in real strength were only to be found in the main position, some 500 yards further on, well out of effective musket shot:

> It is certainly unusual to attempt a sortie at a distance of 900 yards, Therefore the Spanish might have thought himself secure but their own approaches were so improperly guarded, having no banquette or end redans to flank their works, which naturally would lead a General like Eliott to take advantage of such material neglect.[11]

The steep parapet of the San Carlos Battery, pitted already with the strike-marks of round-shot fired from the Rock, was scaled by the company of Hardenberg's Regiment who had lost direction and veered into the path of the centre column (these were the troops fired on by soldiers of the 39th Foot, as they had got so far forward so fast). The whole of the advanced Spanish lines, both complete and those still in preparation, were quickly occupied, together with a few dozen dazed, bruised and wounded prisoners. Scarcely thirty minutes had passed since the British and Hanoverian troops filed out through the barriers. An hour-long spree of smashing the gun and mortar carriages, spiking the firing vents in the pieces (one of which went off accidentally in the process), burning the stores and blowing the powder magazines now began, with remarkably little interference from the main Spanish lines. To add support, the gunners high up in Willis's Battery opened a bombardment, firing over the heads of the sortie troops, while the grenadier companies of De la Motte's and Reden's Regiments moved beyond the forward works, and formed up ready to meet any counter-attack from the Spanish lines stretched across at the neck of the isthmus.

Eliott and a small group of staff officers followed the troops as they moved off, to watch the progress of the operation and, quite possibly, to have their own share in the excitement of the night action. As the forward Spanish works caught alight, Eliott, normally a most undemonstrative man, called out to the soldiers nearby, 'Look round my boys and view how beautiful the Rock appears by the light of this glorious fire.'[12] Brigadier General Ross, however, seemed rather put out that the Governor and his entourage had come so far forward, where they were unduly exposed but had no proper role, and were not at all in the place where they should be. Eliott said to Ross, 'What do you think of this business, is it not something extraordinary?' The rather gruff response was, 'Most extraordinary, to find you here.'[13] Ross then stumped off to oversee the work of demolition in the battery positions, but missed the chance to be handed the key to the main Spanish powder magazine, which Captain Witham gave to Eliott instead. The Spanish officer in charge of the magazine, a captain of artillery named Joseph Barboza, lay gravely wounded at the entrance, having first struck down a soldier of the 73rd Foot with his sword; the young man resolutely refused to be carried from his post to a place of safety by British soldiers, as the powder train was lit that was to send the place sky-high.[14] The unfortunate, but undeniably gallant, officer had already written his report for the night, in which he used the remarkably mistaken and premature phrase, 'Nothing extraordinary had happened.'[15]

The troops engaged in the sortie returned the same way they had come, and got away after suffering remarkably few casualties. Some of the soldiers took the chance to bring back handfuls of the rather straggly vegetables that still grew in the abandoned garden allotments on the isthmus, to supplement their monotonous diet. The gunners in the main Spanish lines at the neck of the isthmus had opened a rather erratic fire with grape-shot, which caused a few losses among the stormers. The sound of horsemen was also heard in the darkness near the vicinity of

Fort St Barbara, and two companies of Hardenberg's Regiment were turned to face that possible threat and support the grenadier companies, but in the end nothing came of it. 'About 40 of the cavalry did come out of the lines, but upon seeing such superior force hurried back again as fast as their horses' legs could carry them.'[16] In any case, it is very unclear what cavalry or dragoons could have achieved before first light.

As the British and Hanoverian troops fell back, Hardenberg's Regiment found that the gate at Forbes Barrier was firmly shut and locked against them, contrary to the orders given for the operation. They had to make their way around the exposed side of the Inundation to get back through the Bayside Barrier instead, while the forward Spanish powder magazines began to blow up in a series of enormous, ground-shaking, detonations:

> The column of fire and smoke which rolled from the Works grandly illuminated the troops and neighbouring objects ... It is impossible by language to describe ... The principal magazines blew up with a tremendous explosion throwing up vast pieces of timber.[17]

By 5am the whole force engaged in the operation was safely back behind the defences of the Rock. They left behind ruined and burning Spanish lines and batteries, where ten 13-inch mortars had been crippled, along with eighteen of the 26-pounders – ordnance estimated at the time to be worth three million pounds sterling, a truly enormous sum by the value of the day. Stores, powder, tools and timber had been heaped up and set alight, the sheltering parapets and palisades broken down in many places and the ditch filled in. These works had taken months to construct, at enormous effort and expense, and they had been spoiled in little more than an hour. The garrison was greatly cheered by the success, and the besiegers, who had clearly been taken completely by surprise, were correspondingly dejected. As if in retaliation, the Spanish gunners in the main lines opened a heavy bombardment on the wrecked Old Town once again, but this fury would not repair the damage done to their forward batteries and trenches. Samuel Ancell wrote the next day, 'The enemy's works burnt very furiously all yesterday afternoon and evening, and are still on fire.'[18] The flames subsided, but the battery positions were seen to be just heaps of sand and broken scorched timber, in the midst of which scattered shells exploded in the heat from time to time.

Eliott warmly commended those who took part in the raid; the Garrison Orders on 27 November ran, 'The bravery and conduct of the whole detachment, officers, seamen and soldiers, on this glorious occasion, surpasses the Governor's utmost acknowledgement.'[19] The losses sustained were very slight – just four killed and twenty-five wounded, including Lieutenant Tweedie of the 12th Foot, who was shot in the thigh, with just one man from Reden's Hanoverians posted as missing. All their arms, implements and equipment had been brought back, together with some booty, although a soldier in the 73rd Foot rather inexplicably seemed to have lost his kilt. Eighteen prisoners were also taken into Gibraltar, and these included two officers – a gunner subaltern named Don Vincente Friza, and a badly hurt German officer, the 22-year-old Baron Helmstadt, who was serving as a captain in the Walloon Guards:

> Baron Helmestadt, having been severely wounded by a musquet shot in one of his knees, was found lying upon the platform of the St Carlos Battery, by two British artillery soldiers, who, moved with generous compassion at his situation resolved to rescue him … They took him up in the Arms, and carried him out of the Battery, where he must soon have perished in the flames.[20]

The two gunners, both from the 2nd Battalion, Royal Artillery – Campbell and Paton – were joined by one of their own officers, Lieutenant Cuppage, in carrying the stricken nobleman to safety. They made their way slowly back to the Rock, and arrived almost an hour after the rest of the sortie had safely returned, their absence having been counted as casualties suffered in the operation. The young nobleman's life was in such danger that the shattered limb had to be amputated to avoid the onset of gangrene.

The Governor wrote to London with an account of the operation in a dispatch carried from the Rock on 12 December in the naval cutter HMS *Unicorn*:

> The force of the enemy in their Lines consisted of 50 or 60 cavalry and 600 infantry composed of Spanish and Walloon Guards, Artillerists, Cassadores [Caçadores – light infantrymen] and their Light Troops, besides the usual body of workmen …
> The vigorous efforts of His Majesty's Troops on every part of

their extensive front was irresistible and the Enemy after a scattering fire of short duration gave way on all sides and abandoned their stupendous works ... Brigadier–General Ross had the Chief Command and conducted the attack with so much judgement ... as highly contributed to the General success.[21]

Eliott skated over the simple fact that most of the Spanish troops were actually fast asleep some way off in their original lines, and gave the distinct impression instead that a strongly held position had been stormed, although he had not actually said so or told an untruth. He discreetly also made no mention of his own personal excursion with his staff officers to see what was going on, and quite rightly Ross was given the credit for what had been a very successful operation. John Drinkwater's own estimate of the strength of the Spanish guard that night in their forward works was that they had 'from the best information, consisted of one captain, three subalterns and seventy-four privates'. Perhaps sufficient for a guard in times of peace, but hardly adequate when at war.[22] Estimates of the numbers in the forward lines that night varied widely, but the Spanish commander reported that 410 of all ranks had comprised the guard – one company each of Militia Grenadiers and Walloon Guards, and three companies of artillerymen. This is closer to Eliott's estimate, but it is quite possible that the officer, mortified at his own failure, was attempting to excuse his neglect by claiming that an adequate guard had been set that night, when this was not actually so.

The lack of numbers on duty in the forward Spanish lines does not detract from the audacity of the Grand Sortie, or the efficient way in which it was carried out. It is probable, though, that observers on the Rock had carefully watched and noted what was the common Spanish practice at night, and deserters, of whom there was always a trickle, would also have brought in similar information. The two most recent deserters questioned by Eliott would have up-to-date information on the duty rosters and strengths in the lines. Had it been thought that the forward batteries were routinely held in real strength after dark, it is doubtful that Eliott would have chanced so many of his slim, increasingly sickly, garrison in the raid. He had calculated the odds, taken the risk, and come through with a fine success. On a sombre note, it was soon rumoured that a number of the guard in the forward

Spanish lines paid for their failure that night with their lives, their executions an example to the rest of the army to be more alert in future.

The success of the sortie was such that the besiegers seemed at first disinclined even to try to repair the damage done by Ross's men. The fires in the ruined works burned themselves out, but the unexploded shells lying around were a disincentive to move too close, and little effort was made for two weeks to see what matériel and ordnance might be salvaged for future use. The stone-built Centre Guard-house had been relatively little damaged, and was re-occupied by Spanish troops early in December, as a forward defensive post to give warning in case the British and Hanoverians came again. As it was, the reappearance of scurvy among the garrison made such a fresh attempt unlikely, even if there had been enough of a worthwhile objective left within practical striking distance. John Drinkwater had calculated at the beginning of the month that, of the 4,527 soldiers and seamen in the garrison, 591 were too sick or injured to attend their duty. Of these, 467 suffered from scurvy, a figure that grew three weeks later to 603. Drinkwater reckoned that the guards, picquets and working parties required each day amounted to 2,500 men. With only about 4,000 troops really fit for duty, this pace of operations could not be sustained for long, even with the besiegers making no obvious preparations to try to storm the place. The disease was threatening the ability to maintain proper watches and duty rosters, and the incidence of sickness appeared to be quickening. Although undoubtedly heartened by the success of the sortie, a mood of bleak, perverse, determination rather than anything more optimistic had settled over the garrison by the year's end.

Despite the good care taken, the young Baron Helmstadt died on 28 December, to the general regret of all those in the garrison who had met him. His body was chivalrously returned to the Spanish lines, where his anxious fiancée, a local girl, was waiting in the vain hope of his safe return. Samuel Ancell wrote rather sadly:

> 29 December. This morning early, died in the naval hospital, Baron Helmstadt, taken prisoner at San Carlos [battery] on the 27th of last month, and who since had a leg amputated, owing to a wound he received by a musket ball … He was young, handsome, and on the point of nuptial celebration with a beautiful lady, born in the province of Andalucia.[23]

The privateer cutters *Lively*, *Viper*, *Flying Fish* and *Dartmouth Tartar* all made their way into Gibraltar in the early weeks of 1782, their captains having contended with contrary winds to lure the blockading Spanish vessels to the eastwards through the Straits, before slipping past and into harbour. The garrison, as ever with such impudent displays of superior seamanship, were cheered by the exploit, but less pleased by the very high prices the privateer captains charged for the goods they brought in, with tea selling at £4 for a pound, well beyond the slim purses of most in Gibraltar by this time.

Major General James Murray, the commander of the garrison in Minorca, had command of only four weak infantry battalions (two British – the 51st Foot and the 61st Foot, and two Hanoverian – Prinz Ernst's and Godacher's – together with a handful of seamen serving ashore, about 2,700 all ranks). There was little that Murray could do when a powerful force 8,000 strong under Louis de Balba de Berton, the 63-year-old Comte de Crillon (a French officer in the service of Madrid), landed on the island. Eliott had already kept hold of the 73rd Foot for the defence of Gibraltar, but, given the strength of the French and Spanish forces involved, the result in Minorca was probably a foregone conclusion. Despite his lack of numbers, Murray spurned an offer to submit on generous terms and his troops resisted for five gruelling months, mounting at least one sharp counter-attack that took de Crillon quite by surprise and captured twenty-two prisoners. The 600 exhausted, starving, and scurvy-riven survivors of the garrison, weak and unable to man their posts in Fort St Philip, were forced to submit on 5 February 1782, and allowed the honours of war, in recognition of their fine resistance. A British military surgeon, Dr Beatson, wrote of the capitulation: 'A more noble, nor a more tragic scene was never exhibited, than that of the march of the garrison of St Philip's, through the Spanish and French armies.'[24] De Crillon was not alone as he wept on seeing their miserable condition, when the ragged British and Hanoverian soldiers and sailors crept and staggered past him. For all Murray's stout defence, Minorca was lost for ever to Great Britain, and it was fairly certain that reinforcements would be sent to take a hand in the operations against Gibraltar. The acclaimed victor of the conquest of Minorca, would go to take over the command of the siege operations where speedy success was confidently anticipated in both Madrid and Paris.

It had been known for some time that many of the British guns on the Rock could not bear directly on the Spanish works, and were accordingly rather ineffective. When the gun crews tried to haul their pieces around to get a better field of view, they became exposed to counter-battery fire. Lieutenant George Koehler, Royal Artillery (who had come to Gibraltar in Darby's convoy), devised a 'depress gun-carriage', an ingenious device that enabled the muzzle of the artillery piece to be lowered by 20 degrees (sometimes more), to enable the gunners to fire down from the heights of the Rock onto the siege lines across the isthmus. The new gun-carriage also allowed the piece to be swung around for reloading, without exposing the crew very much to enemy fire. An impressive demonstration of the capabilities of the novel weapon was held for Eliott's benefit on 15 February 1782, and the St Carlos Battery was hit with twenty-eight out of the first thirty rounds fired. Whether any lasting or significant damage was done was rather less certain, but the spectacle certainly cheered the onlookers.

The same day, the aptly named *Governor Eliott*, sailing out of Cork, managed to go aground on the northern side of the Old Mole, due to some inexplicable miscalculation by her commander, Captain Sam Sheldon, who appeared to think that the nearest Spanish batteries were no longer in action. The brig's crew were brought off safely in boats, while the gunners fired on the ship, expending a considerable amount of powder and shot, but without doing very much damage. Don Barcelo had worked his squadron back into the approaches to Gibraltar Bay and re-imposed the blockade, and Samuel Ancell commented, 'Some of the enemy's boats having been drove near the garrison, the batteries at Europa discharged a few shot at them, but plying their oars briskly, they got off without any injury.'[25] A heartening success was the arrival on 23 February of the armed brig *Mercury*, laden with fresh fruit and lemons. The vessel fought her way gamely past a Spanish frigate and a xebec with her most welcome cargo, particularly useful in the treatment of scurvy. This voyage was the product of a neat deception as the commander, Lieutenant Heighton, had sailed from Gibraltar in January, apparently bound for home. So convincing was this declared intention that some civilian passengers were on board, eager to escape the privations of the siege. However, Heighton put into Lisbon, and having filled his hold with the valuable cargo of citrus fruit, without saying a word of his intentions, sailed back to the Rock, very much to the surprise of his disconsolate passengers, who had really been hoping to see the cliffs and beaches of the south coast of England instead.

All the Spanish ships in the Bay and at Algeciras, were dressed overall in full colours that day, and salute guns fired, in obvious celebration of a success – it was not difficult for the garrison to guess the reason for this. On 1 March a Spanish officer under flag of truce came over the flat ground of the isthmus with the dismal news that the British garrison in Minorca had submitted a few weeks earlier. Eliott could now expect the pace of operations against his garrison to quicken, but just the following day, the British gunners managed to set fire to a new 13-gun battery that had just been completed. The Spanish artillerymen showed great spirit in putting the flames out with buckets of sand while still under bombardment from the Rock, and they earned grudging admiration from the watchers in the garrison for their courage.

On 23 March John Drinkwater recorded a particularly unfortunate incident in the daily round of bombardment and counter-bombardment:

> A shot came through one of the capped embrasures on Princess Amelia's battery, took the legs off two men belonging to the 72nd and 73rd Regiments, one leg off a soldier of the 73rd, and wounded another man in both legs; thus four men had seven legs taken off and wounded by one shot.[26]

Lieutenant William Cuppage, who had helped to bring in Baron Helmstadt after the Great Sortie, was gravely injured by a shell that exploded prematurely in the muzzle of the artillery-piece as it was being fired. On 10 April a shell fired from a Spanish battery landed among the guard at the Land-Port as it was being mounted, killing the inspecting officer, Lieutenant Whitham of the 12th Foot. On the other hand, a certain grim humour could be had when under fire, as when a gunner called out in amazement to his comrades that a Spanish round-shot had just grazed his nose as it went past. They watched him curiously, but in growing disappointment, expecting at any moment that he would drop dead from the concussion to his brain. He lived on, and interest in the much-embellished anecdote of his narrow escape quickly faded away, as he was plainly not about to expire.

At the end of March the frigates HMS *Apollo* and *Cerberus* convoyed in four transports bringing the 97th Regiment of Foot under the command of Colonel Stanton to reinforce the garrison. Soon afterwards, the frigate *Success* escorted in the merchantman *Vernon*, after fighting a Spanish frigate to a standstill and boarding the ship, which then had to be abandoned and burned as Don Barcelo's squadron approached. It was soon found that the new recruits of the 97th were not in very good condition at all; they lost 100 men to sickness within a month of arrival on the Rock, while their commanding officer died of sunstroke. Still, it was a relief that the severity and incidence of scurvy began to abate once again, and by early May there were only thirty-three invalids with that particular sickness still in hospital. *Vernon* also brought in a number of disassembled gunboats, which when reconstructed and manned could be put to use fighting the jabecquillas that prowled Gibraltar Bay.

Less heartening was the capture on 7 May of three transports, *Thompson*, *Loyal Briton* and *Valiant*, homeward bound from Gibraltar, which were taken into Algeciras as prizes. However, a week or so later, three more merchantmen laden with gunpowder and round-shot bluffed their way through the blockade by flying French colours and turning into Gibraltar rather than Algeciras at the last moment. A colourful diversion was also provided when a xebec-rigged privateer coming out of Leghorn, the *St George*, slipped past the blockading squadron and put into harbour on 25 May 1782. On board was a Corsican officer, Señor Leonara, and twelve compatriots, all veterans of fighting the French in their homeland and now volunteering for service under Eliott. They were joined soon afterwards by other Corsicans, who proved to be rather argumentative, with one man being killed in a knife-fight. They provided a very useful addition to the bayonet strength of the garrison, all the same, and a separate company under the command of a Captain Commandant Leonetti was formed in early August.

That same month, one of the most novel features of the Great Siege began. General Eliott had been discussing with Colonel Green, his Chief of Engineers, how to bring more effective fire on the Spanish batteries on the isthmus. Lieutenant Koehler's depress gun-carriage innovation had helped, but the problem had become more acute as the Spanish entrenchments edged closer once more. Sergeant Major Henry Ince of the Company of Soldier-Artificers overheard the

Governor's comments, and stepped forward to suggest that a tunnel could be dug through the solid rock, from Farringdon's Battery (Willis's) to an outcrop known as the Notch, and so establish a battery higher up on the sheer North Face than had been possible up to then. Eliott was taken with the idea, and gave Ince instructions to begin work straight away, with a party of twelve soldiers (later increased to eighteen), all of whom had some mining experience. Supervised by Lieutenant Eveleigh, an aide-de-camp to the Governor, the work began on 22 May.

The initial gallery, eighty-two feet long, eight feet wide and eight feet high, was complete by mid-July, and a powder charge used to blow out an opening to give ventilation as Ince and his men worked. The report of the explosion was so loud that the entire Spanish camp turned out to see what was going on. This opening also proved to be a very useful embrasure for a 24-pounder gun, with a hollow scooped out of the rock to the rear to allow the piece to recoil fully. To their surprise, the Spanish gunners soon found themselves being fired on from this new and novel direction, and by September a further four gun positions had been constructed in this way. The miners eventually reached the Notch some months after operations came to an end, and they hollowed out St George's Hall, with embrasures for seven guns. Although a lasting reminder of the ingenuity shown during the Great Siege, the tunnels had little practical effect, as hostilities were coming to an end before they were ready for effective use.[27]

A more surprising and improbable proposal, on the Spanish side of the lines, was a notion to build a vast artificial mound, sufficiently high for batteries to be mounted which could dominate the guns of the Gibraltar garrison. Although the precise cubic content of such an enormous project and the time necessary for its construction were carefully calculated, rather unsurprisingly the curious idea was not taken forward. Gas warfare was also considered: 'Filling grenades with some substance so noxious that when they exploded within the walls they would either poison the besieged or force them to take flight.'[28] However, Samuel Ancell recorded the rumour that another new and novel weapon was being prepared for use against the Rock: 'A deserter from the Volunteers of Aragon came in, and confirms a former account of ships being prepared for the purpose of attacking the garrison, lined with cork and junk to prevent the penetration of shot.'[29] Battering ships of massive force, great floating batteries in effect, were being prepared to attack the garrison on the Rock.

An Equal Share of Glory

The Spanish entrenchments snaked their stealthy way forward once more, but a bombardment by Eliott's gunners late in July produced few results, apparently not slowing the work very much at all at that range. So, deciding against any further waste of powder and shot, other than to keep his opponents on the watch, the Spanish workmen and pioneers were allowed to come on, unimpeded but closely observed. By allowing this work to continue, Eliott was, in effect, trying to draw them on into an artillery killing zone, well within the effective range of massed and well-sited batteries on the Rock. The idea came to nothing in the end, as entrenching work on the isthmus gradually dwindled, and the attention of the Spanish and French commanders moved instead to the preparations for a great seaward attack.

To combat the persistent attentions of the Spanish jabecquillas – Mrs Kate Upton's 'Infernal spit-fires' – the disassembled gunboats brought in by the transport *Vernon* were put together, and by 4 June 1782 twelve of these useful craft were in service at the New Mole, stirringly named *Revenge*, *Spitfire*, *Terror*, *Defiance*, *Dreadnought*, *Europa*, *Thunder*, *Fury*, *Vengeance*, *Resolution*, *Terrible* and *Scourge*. Each one was armed with a single 18 or 24-pounder gun in the bow and manned by a crew of twenty-one seamen drawn from the under-employed warships HMS *Brilliant*, *Porcupine* and *Speedwell*. They were soon in action against the Spanish cruisers off Europa Point, before assistance came from the rest of the blockading squadron.

Many small-scale battles were fought in the Bay between the rival gunboats, and the freedom of action hitherto enjoyed by Don Barcelo was noticeably reduced. The British boats also scouted the margins of the Bay at night, peering into Algeciras harbour and Sandy Bay to see what was going on. They observed the arrival of a fresh French squadron of twelve ships under the command of Admiral Gleichen, together with transports carrying more French soldiers, veterans of the capture of Minorca, to add their weight to the siege. The combined Spanish and

French forces, now about 35,000 strong, were ranged against Eliott and his stubborn garrison of just 7,500 men (when the actually ineffective sick, lazy and wounded languishing in hospital were included).

The novel notion of a battering ships' attack on Gibraltar was the brainchild of Jean-Claude-Eléonor Le Michaud, the Chevalier d'Arçon, a distinguished 49-year-old French engineer officer. The vessels to be used in the attempt were ten old and obsolete hulks, ranging from 600 tons to 1,400 tons, which would be adapted and reinforced to become what were, in effect, powerful floating batteries, intended to overwhelm at close range the defences on the Rock. The arrival off Algeciras of the vessels ready to be converted into battering ships was noted by Samuel Ancell when he wrote to his brother on 9 May:

> This forenoon, arrived from the westward, one line of battle ship, convoying eight large store-ships or Indiamen. From the appearance of their rigging and sides, which is dry and shabby, and having but few hands on board, we cannot imagine from what place they have arrived or what occasion brought them in here ...
> It is currently reported that they are lined with cork, and are to be converted into batteries, but most people think they are more fit for fire-wood than attacking a fortress.[1]

More Spanish and French warships came into the Bay in the coming weeks, together with transports bringing more reinforcements for the besieging forces. It really seemed that, as blockade had not succeeded in reducing the garrison, a great effort to take the Rock by main force was at last in preparation.

D'Arçon's plans for the preparation of the battering ships were certainly ingenious, and intended to make them proof from counter-battery fire. Some of the rigging was removed, and the open upper decks of the vessels were roofed over with sloping stout timbers, rope netting and wet hides. The side of the ships which would be exposed to hostile fire were reinforced with additional bracing and thick timber beams, with a layer of sand and one of cork sandwiched in between. More imaginatively, an ingenious system of water pumps and pipes was installed so that any fire that broke out when in action could be quickly doused by the crews before it became a real danger. The additional weight of this equipment and reinforcing of the exposed side was counterbalanced by carefully shifting the stone ballast in the holds towards the less exposed side, so that the battering ships should not be in peril of heeling over and capsizing when under way.

With so much attention focused on the preparation of the battering ships for action, the long weeks of summer, with oppressive heat and little wind, passed rather quietly, apart from the occasional arrival at the Rock of supplies aboard blockade-runners, and the daily bombardment and counter-bombardment, slowly declining in intensity but each day taking its grim toll of casualties, dead and broken men, and not infrequently the women and their unfortunate children. Mid-morning on 11 June a Spanish mortar bomb scored a direct hit on the expense powder magazine of Princess Anne's Battery. The resulting enormous explosion, with some 100 barrels of powder going up all together, seemed to shake the Rock to its very core, killing fourteen men and wounding another fifteen. A larger magazine nearby had the door blown clean off but fortunately it did not also detonate. The Spanish gunners stood on their parapets to cheer the success, but the Battery was back in action, albeit in reduced form, within a few days. Two weeks later, Samuel Ancell recalled that it was 'All quiet on the isthmus excepting now and then a shot for diversion, which sometimes we return and sometimes not ... little fire from the enemy [but] the floating batteries are forwarded with incredible expedition.'[2]

The weather remained oppressively hot; dull routine mixed with fleeting danger was the daily norm. Interest was attracted to a duel fought with small-swords between Captain Witham and Lieutenant Burleigh over some imagined slight to one or the other, but there was valour as well as such whimsical fancies. Caleb Hartley, a gunner, was working in a magazine to fit fuses to 5 and 6-inch shells on 8 July, when one of the fuses suddenly burst alight in his hand. John Drinkwater recalled:

> With the most astonishing coolness he carried out the lighted shell, and threw it where it could do little or no harm; and two seconds had scarcely elapsed before it disploded. If the shell had burst in the laboratory, it is almost certain that the whole would have been blown up; when the loss in fixed ammunition, fuzes, etc etc, would have been irreparable, exclusive of the damage which the fortifications would have suffered from the explosion, and the lives that might have been lost. He was handsomely rewarded by the Governor.[3]

In the wider war, away from the Rock, Admiral de Grasse had managed to slip his fleet across the Atlantic while the Royal Navy was busy resupplying Gibraltar. He had done a lot of mischief to British interests in the West Indies, but cheerful news was received in Gibraltar at about this time of Admiral Rodney's stirring success at the Battle of the Saintes, when he famously broke de Grasse's battle-line courtesy of a sudden change in the wind.

The recovery of Minorca had been a longstanding aim for Spain, second only in importance to that of Gibraltar, and the Duc de Crillon (as he had become after the victory on the island) was very much favoured in Madrid. Fresh from his triumph, he had promptly taken over the command of the rather lame attempt to seize Gibraltar.[4] So bright were the apparent prospects for early victory that on 15 August 1782 two French Princes of the Blood – Louis XVI's young brothers, the Comte d'Artois (who would become King Charles X of France, 1824–30), and the Duc de Bourbon (Louis XVIII, 1814–15) – came to watch the operations. Before long, the princes were joined by numerous noble Spanish and French sightseers, both male and female in all their finery, well provisioned as for a picnic, and eager to see, from a prudently safe distance, the downfall of the impudent fortress that had held out for so long. A kind of grandstand, decked in bright colours, was erected so that the guests could view the thrilling spectacle in suitable comfort. On 19 August Governor Eliott received a letter from de Crillon, who wrote from the camp at Buenavista:

> His Royal Highness the Comte d'Artois, who has received permission from the King his brother to assist at the siege, as volunteer in the Combined [Spanish and French] Army, of which their Most Christian and Catholic Majesties have honoured me with the command, arrived in this camp on the 15th instant. This young Prince has been pleased, in passing through Madrid, to take charge of some letters, which had been sent to the capital from this place, and which are addressed to persons belonging to your garrison; His Royal Highness has desired that I should transmit them to you … His Highness the Duc de Bourbon, who arrived twenty-four hours after the Comte d'Artois, desires also that I should assure you of his particular esteem.[5]

Along with the letters, the Comte d'Artois had asked that a selection of fresh fruit, ice and vegetables be sent as a gift, knowing that the British commander ate no meat: 'Permit me, Sir, to offer a few trifles for your table, of which I am sure you stand in need.' Eliott was rather embarrassed by this gesture, and asked de Crillon that no more such gifts should be sent, as in any case, he shared any additional rations he came by, however obtained, with his troops. 'I confess,' he wrote,

> I make it a point of honour to partake both of plenty and scarcity in common with the lowest of my brave fellow-soldiers. This furnishes me with an excuse for the liberty I now take, of entreating your Excellency not to heap any more favours on me of this kind.

On a more practical note, away from the social niceties of the commanding generals, the British gunners had been practising with the technique of heating round-shot in specially constructed ovens near their battery positions, until the projectiles were glowing red-hot. Fire at sea was always the worst fear, and the potential effectiveness of the use of this fearsome weapon against wooden ships and boats was plain.

On 14 July, a deserter came in from the Spanish lines, with news that the battering ships would be ready for action by the end of August, and it was also noticed that heavier artillery pieces were being hauled into position in the Spanish works. One of the newly arrived French generals was taken by a Spanish officer to a forward battery, so that he could inspect the defences of the Rock more clearly. The British gunners greeted this impertinence with a well-aimed shot that made both officers duck down rather quickly, although no injury was suffered. The Frenchman quickly recovered his composure, and responded to the shot by doffing his hat in an elegant salute to the artillerymen, before moving smartly off to a more sheltered spot. The garrison gunners, impressed with his nonchalance, gave him a cheer.

Likened by one soldier to oblong water-borne haystacks, the battering ships were protected in harbour by a defensive boom over 2,000 yards long. They were, in effect, floating batteries and, as such, not a particularly novel innovation. It was hoped that their employment would enable the besiegers to engage those batteries on the comparatively exposed western side of Gibraltar, guns that were otherwise safe from bombardment. The handling of such clumsy vessels, with the foremast and much of the standing rigging removed, would probably not be too great a handicap in the comparatively sheltered waters of the Bay. To have any chance of real success, however, the operation of the ships would have to be made in concert with amphibious landing parties, and aggressive action by the land forces on the isthmus – perhaps a sudden fierce bombardment and an infantry sortie to rush the defences at the Barriers and the Land-Port Gate under cover of darkness, and in that way gain a lodgement on the Rock itself. A bold enterprise to overwhelm such stout defences inevitably required a fair measure of daring and acceptance of risk, but also that the various parties employed should work well together in a carefully co-ordinated effort.

The plan submitted by De Crillon for approval by the King in Madrid, made it clear that he envisaged an all-arms attack, concurrent massive bombardment by land and sea, closely followed by infantry attacks across the isthmus and amphibious landings on the western shore of the Rock:

> The assault will be conducted in the following manner: Brigadier Don Ventura Moreno will command the fire of the fleet. The vanguard of the combined squadron will be commanded by Senor Cordoba, and among the divisions that compose it will be included the 3rd [division] of 12 fire-proof ships, which will anchor in Algeciras, until Senor Alvarez completes the 60 paces of internment opposite the fortress. Our ships will then attack … their fire being supported by that of the gun and mortar-boats and bomb ketches, which will hold themselves in readiness to support where it may be required. At a given signal the fire from our whole line will open with that of the intrenchment, which will not cease until a breach shall have been made [when] the Duke de Crillon will notify to the governor the surrender of the fortress, and should he consent to the capitulation, the preliminaries will be arranged conceding him military honours.

The reference to the new entrenchments refers to the works which would be thrown up under cover of night, the construction of which would entail the placing at night of over one million sandbags.

> If he [Eliott] persist in the defence, the operations will follow in the following manner. The fire by sea and land will protect the disembarkation of our troops on the flanks of the advance. The

> boats conveying them will be covered by large planks on hinges, which on unfolding will fall on the moles on the right ... The troops will advance along these in the following order: 11 companies of Grenadiers of about 70 men each, and as many more of Chasseurs with three companies of dragoons, the whole under the command of Senor Cagigal ... Two battalions of Volunteers of Catalonia will form the flying troops to form a support where it may be necessary, and to strengthen either flank ... When the disembarkation of the troops, or part of them, shall have been executed, the boats carrying the fascines, powder-saucisses, gabions, panniers, pick-axes etc., will be sent forward in order that they may cover themselves as the disembarkation proceeds, keeping up at the same time a lively fire along with the rest of the army.[6]

This was all well thought out and as it should be, but the French commander, under pressure from Madrid to get on with things, would disregard his own good intentions before long.

The ships, heavily encumbered with an estimated total of 200,000 cubic feet of additional timber planking, and with their main batteries only mounted on the port side, certainly proved to be awkward and unhandy, even in quiet waters. A demonstration of one of the vessels was held for the benefit of the Comte d'Artois and his brother, but the ship proved incapable of turning in the light current and had, rather ignominiously, to be towed back to Algeciras by the more reliable gunboats.

> The ten batteries had been built so as to present to the enemy only a strip three feet thick lined with slats and kept constantly flooded with water by an artificial device. It was confidently expected that red-hot cannonballs would be extinguished on the spot where they fell.[7]

D'Arçon was concerned at an apparent lack of co-operation, and even interest, among some Spanish officers, most noticeably the governor of Algeciras: 'A half-witted man,' he wrote, 'uniformly inept and full of the most vile prejudices.'[8] However this might have been, others were not too enthusiastic over the battering-ships project, expressing doubts quite clearly: 'The plan is impossible. You cannot oppose batteries made of wood, which will undoubtedly catch fire, to those on land. Everyone knows that cannon-balls fired from a ship have less power."[9]

Most critically, de Crillon had little faith in the ability of the battering ships to subdue the defences on the Rock. This is clearly shown in a letter which he left in Madrid, only to be opened once the attack was actually under way:

> On leaving for Gibraltar, I declare that I accept the command which His Majesty has done me the honour of conferring upon me, to carry out the plan with the floating batteries against the fortress. I promise to assist M. d'Arçon by every means until the moment when the batteries have begun their attack … If, contrary to my opinion, the fortress is taken by the effect of the said batteries, and the assault following on their actions, all the glory of this feat of arms shall go to M. d'Arçon, the French engineer who is the author of the plan. I also declare that, should the floating batteries not prove successful, no reproach can be made to me, since I have taken no part in the project.[10]

He was plainly making his excuses at the outset if matters went wrong, instead of frankly saying that the effort was probably futile, and the note does him no credit. The difficulty was that the King and his ministers in Madrid were eagerly looking forward to the grand attack and, buoyed up by the recent capture of Minorca and the sycophantic assurances of those at Court, everyone was now confident of success. Don Barcelo, obstinate and persistent, had been superseded by Admiral Don Cordoba, who had succeeded so well in capturing the huge British convoy off the Azores. He had gone on to seize a second convoy in the English Channel, and was acknowledged as a naval commander of undoubted ability and much in favour after such recent triumphs. However, Don Cordoba proved to be less comfortable operating in the tricky and confined waters of the Straits and Bay of Gibraltar, and it might have been better to leave things in Don Barcelo's rough but capable hands.

The garrison on the Rock watched the preparations in Algeciras harbour with professional and detached interest, but although on the alert, they seemed to be little concerned at what was apparently intended. John Drinkwater recalled:

> The enemy seemed entirely to have overlooked the nature of the force which was opposed to them; for though the garrison

scarcely consisted of more than 7,000 effective men, including the marine brigade, they forgot they were now veterans in this service, had long been habituated to the effects of artillery, and were, by degrees, prepared for the arduous conflict that awaited them.[11]

However, the guns along the North Face were now routinely kept loaded with grape-shot or canister at all times, in case of a sudden Spanish infantry sortie across the Neutral Ground. This had seemed unlikely until now, but on the night of 15 August Spanish pioneers and workmen constructed a new advanced trench, over 500 yards in length, and a battery, under cover of the dark hours. It was as if some attempt to rush the defences was in preparation, and the vast amount of material necessary to construct the trench and the linking works

The Spanish battering ships, all of which had guns in reserve to replace those that might be disabled during the action, were as follows:

Ship	No. of guns	Commander
Pastora	21	Rear Admiral Don Bonaventura Moreno
Talla Piedra	21	Prince of Nassau-Sieghen
Paula Prima	21	Don Gayetana Langara
El Rosario	19	Don Francisco Xavier Manos
San Christobal	18	Don Frederico Gravilo
Principe Carlos	11	Don Antonio Basuela
San Juan	9	Don Joseph Angeler
Paula Secunda	9	Don Pablo de Cosa
Santa Anna	7	Don Joseph Goicoechea
Los Dolores	6	Don Pedro Sanchez

had been brought forward in secret, and quite unnoticed by the garrison. Spanish boats were observed taking soundings off the Old Mole under cover of darkness on 7 September, and shots were fired to keep them at a distance, but the salvo did no noticeable damage in the poor light. D'Arçon, anxious to obtain as much information at first hand as he could, was in one of the boats on this nocturnal expedition, but the fire from the Rock was sufficient to ensure that the reconnaissance was unable to determine the precise depth of the Bay at this important spot.

Eliott had formed a plan to bombard the forward Spanish lines with a potent mixture of inflammable carcasses, red-hot shot, and Mercier's short-fused air-burst shells, both to distract de Crillon's attentions from the preparation of the battering ships, and to reduce the ability of the land-based gunners to support any naval attack. Early on the morning of Sunday, 8 September 1782, the deputy Governor, Lieutenant General Sir Robert Boyd (who was obliged to sit in a chair on account of his enfeebled health), gave the order, and all the British batteries from the Old Mole to the lofty Rock Gun roared into fiery life. A prolonged and heavy artillery assault began on the forward Spanish lines at the western side of the isthmus. There, a new work known as the Mahon Battery (named, presumably, in honour of the recent success on Minorca) had recently been erected. Samuel Ancell wrote to his brother, 'We began a furious cannonade of red hot balls upon the enemy's Mahon Battery, and their lines of approach.'[12]

Despite the ferocity of the British fire, the Spanish and French gunners behaved with great courage, and gave back shot for shot, although their counter-bombardment was ineffective by comparison. As the day wore on, it could be seen from the Rock that the Mahon Battery was in ruins, with fires raging through the positions despite the best efforts of the gun-crews to extinguish the flames; the nearby San Carlos and San Martin Batteries were also badly damaged. Ancell went on, 'The foe withstood our fire with intrepidity. Their works were blazing in several places, and strewed over with mangled limbs and dead bodies ... a horrid scene of great slaughter.' A French officer who watched the bombardment of the Mahon Battery afterwards wrote in despair:

The heart is rent with the sight and groans of the dying and wounded, whom the soldiers are this moment carrying away; the number makes a man shudder; and I am told that in other parts of the lines, which are not within view of my post, the numbers are still greater.[13]

The sudden duel had been decisively won on this occasion by the garrison, and the Spanish and French gunners in the forward positions on the isthmus had suffered some 300 killed and wounded in the action, while the loss on the Rock was trifling by comparison. No fewer than 5,543 shot and shell had been fired by the garrison gunners, about ten rounds each minute of the bombardment. The operation had been a real success, conducted by Boyd and the officers supervising the firing with precision and skill, inflicting serious damage and casualties at little cost, and greatly to their credit. As the order to cease firing was given in the late afternoon, the Deputy Governor left his chair and gently limped to his quarters, while his officers waved their hats in salute and the sweating, smoke-grimed, gunners lustily cheered him on his way.

Despite this, two signal rockets were suddenly fired from the Spanish entrenchments at first light the next morning. A heavy bombardment began from the surviving batteries ranged across the neck of the isthmus and along the adjacent coastline. Some 230 artillery pieces and mortars were counted as being in action, although the nearest batteries to the Rock, after the damage inflicted the previous day, unsurprisingly contributed little to the effort. The heaviest fire was directed at the line wall north of the King's Bastion, and, as the morning wore on, nine Spanish and French warships, using a light breeze, made their stately way southwards along the length of the wall towards Europa Point, adding the weight of the fire of their own broadsides to the bombardment.[14] Spanish gunboats and mortar-boats, usually most active and dangerous at night, also attacked the bastion, but these were soon driven off by the return fire, with Eliott's gunners making good use of their heated round-shot, gaining further useful practice in the difficult procedures necessary with this dangerous weapon, while under comparatively slight pressure. While all this was going on, an audacious Algerine privateer, laden with provisions and cattle, slipped nimbly into harbour with its cargo, quite unscathed, although fired on by the nearest batteries.

The Spanish and French bombardment grew in intensity and

continued throughout the following days, appearing to be an attempt to wear down the capabilities and energy of the British gunners, in anticipation of some great effort by the besieging forces. John Drinkwater wrote, 'They hoped probably to confound and overwhelm us, by presenting to us destruction under such various forms and by the enormous quantity which they poured in.'[15] Samuel Ancell remembered that preparations also seemed to be under way to mount an attack across the sands of the isthmus, as gaps were made in the palisades fringing the forward trenches, wide enough for eight men to advance abreast at a time. For unknown reasons these preparations never came to anything, but he commented on the grisly effects of the bombardment:

> I observed a soldier before me, laying on the ground, and his head somewhat raised, and supported on his elbow; I ran to him, imagining the man had life, and lifted him up, when such a sight was displayed to my view, that I think I shall never forget. A 26lb ball had gone through his body, and his entrails as they hung out of the orifice, were of a most disagreeable resemblance.[16]

On Thursday, 12 September, a combined Spanish and French naval squadron sailed into the Bay, a most imposing sight, forty-four ships-of-the-line, with frigates in support. This seems to have been yet another attempt to overawe the garrison and present Eliott with the opportunity to submit with honour in the face of a vastly superior force.

A council of war was held that evening, attended by de Crillon, Rear Admiral Don Bonaventura Moreno (who had command of the flotilla of battering ships), and d'Arçon. Feeling that his reputation was at some risk from the delay, while privately doubting that success was to be had, de Crillon urged that the attack should be made at the earliest opportunity. D'Arçon protested that the arrangements for the operation were still incomplete, in particular that the battering ships were not properly caulked and were leaky as a result, and that proper trials in open water had yet to be carried out. Don Moreno shared the concerns, but seemed inclined to stand aloof, and took little constructive part in the discussions. De Crillon impatiently waved the concerns away – the attack was to be made without further delay, and he declared that he would have the admiral replaced if he did not comply. The meeting broke up in an atmosphere of disharmony, and

Don Moreno went off to give orders to his captains.

Early on 13 September the leading battering ship, *Pastora*, with Don Moreno and his staff officers on board, set out from Algeciras and came over on a light north-westerly breeze towards the Rock, dropping anchor at 9.45am about 500 yards off the middle point of the King's Bastion. The next in line, *Talla Piedra*, with d'Arçon on board, drew up close behind. Within a quarter of an hour or so, the other battering ships had closed up, although some clearly found difficulty in getting to their allotted station: 'The batteries took up positions different from those assigned to them. Only the leading two stationed themselves on the spot to which they had been ordered.'[17] Three ships, *Paula Prima*, *El Rosario* and *San Juan*, drew ahead to anchor pretty well where intended, but the rearmost five ships grounded on a sandbank and remained stuck fast, too far distant from the shore for their fire to be effective. It appeared that d'Arçon and his officers had not managed to sound the depth of the water very well on their reconnaissance, or if they had, they had not briefed the commanders of the ships with enough care.

Despite the scattered positioning of the ships, the Spanish gunners opened a heavy cannonade on the shore batteries. The great attack by the battering ships, for all the imperfections of the plan and preparations, deployed 212 brass guns of large calibre against the defenders. At first the crews were firing low, wasting their shot on the shore-line, but soon corrected their aim, and gradually all the ships had added their weight to the bombardment. 'The floating batteries have just brought up between the Old Mole and King's Bastion, within 500 yards of the walls,' Samuel Ancell wrote, 'the garrison have begun firing at them.'[18] The gunners on the Rock were in action, engulfed in flying shot, razor-sharp stone splinters, and billowing clouds of acrid smoke. Casualties quickly began to mount up, particularly in the batteries to the north of the King's Bastion. With both land and sea batteries hard at work, over 400 pieces of artillery were in thunderous close-quarter action, the gun crews gallantly standing to their pieces and returning their opponents' fire, shot for shot, and with ever increasing rapidity.

John Drinkwater wrote that the fire from the King's Bastion and adjoining batteries seemed to have disappointingly little effect, as even the shot of the heavy 32-pounders was deflected from the reinforced hull sides, or rolled off the protective covering over the upper decks. 'The wonderful construction of the ships seemed to bid defiance to the power of the heaviest ordnance.'[19] However, the fatal flaw in the French and Spanish plan was becoming evident. It was apparent before long that the attack by the battering ships would be the only major effort made against the garrison that day – there was certainly some artillery support from the batteries on the isthmus, but no sign at all of either an infantry advance across the sands, or landing parties of marines setting out in boats from the shores across the Bay. The ships' crews would have to fight and win their gunnery contest almost alone. Even if they did so, it was difficult to see what they would have achieved, and what then was to be done to make the most of their success. Death and destruction along the exposed western shoreline of the Rock might have been inflicted, but when the ships drew off, which they must surely do at some point to replenish their stocks of powder and shot, Eliott would have a relatively untroubled breathing space in which to re-establish his batteries from the stock of spare cannon (and somewhat less numerous replacement gunners) he had in reserve for such a purpose. Any attack from the Bay, if made on its own without real support, had little chance of achieving very much, and every gun of the Rock that could be brought to bear was pounding the ships with relatively little hindrance from the Spanish land batteries. 'The whole firing at once from the land-side and that of the sea, afforded the most terrible and horrid spectacle.'[20]

The position taken up by the battering ships was certainly not ideal. Not only were they anchored further offshore than originally intended, but the leading five ships were well ahead of the following group, which remained grounded on the sandbank. The result was that the two groups engaged the shore batteries with less concentrated fire than was intended, wastefully dispersing the weight of metal aimed at the King's Bastion and the adjacent batteries, although noticeable damage was certainly being inflicted:

> The crews on the battering ships were tortured by the heat and thirst, and by the wearying labour of keeping their guns in constant action. The protection added to the ships worked fairly well and their casualties were, for some time, very light, despite the heavy counter-battery work from the gunners on the Rock. All the same, their own efforts appeared to be in vain, and the weight of shot directed at the ships gradually increased in volume

rather than noticeably diminishing – it was, though, still rather ineffective, and many of the gunners on the Rock despaired for some time of being able to drive off the battering ships.[21]

Shortly after midday the ships' crews had to face a fresh hazard: Eliott's gunners had prepared their heated shot, the 'roast potatoes' in the jaunty jargon of the soldiery, and the projectiles were glowing red-hot in the ovens. The process had taken longer than anticipated, but now at last they could be gingerly taken by the gunners' mates in sand-filled wheelbarrows to the waiting guns; wads damped with water were thrust down the barrels to prevent premature explosions, and then the heated shot was rammed home ready for firing. This technique was laborious and fraught with hazards, but the gunners had practised their drills, and at about midday the batteries on the King's and Orange Bastions opened a heavy fire with their 'roast potatoes', concentrating at first on the larger ships, *Pastora*, *Talla Piedra* and *Paula Prima*. Nonetheless, John Drinkwater wrote that this still seemed to have little effect:

> No sooner did any smoke appear, than, with admirable intrepidity, men were observed applying water from their engines within, to those places where the smoke issued ... Even the artillery[men] themselves, at this period, had their doubts of the effect of the red-hot shot, which began to be made about twelve, but were not general till between one and two o'clock.[22]

Observers clustered around the Queen of Spain's Chair could see that the entire western side of the Rock was wreathed in swirling smoke, shot through with flashes of gunfire. The gunners on the battering ships kept to their grim duty, and maintained the fierce duel with Eliott's artillerymen (who were relieved at regular intervals by sailors of Lieutenant Trentham's Marine brigade) with great energy well into the early evening. It became a test of grim endurance, for the gun crews on both sides were labouring at their pieces in the heat and sulphurous smoke, deafened and dazed by the repeated discharges of the cannonade, parched and tormented by thirst.

The stout reinforced planking and the wet hides cladding the battering ships, together with ingenious water pumping systems, appeared to be proof against this deadly fire. Courageous seamen were occasionally seen clambering onto the sloping roofs of the ships to kick and roll off round-

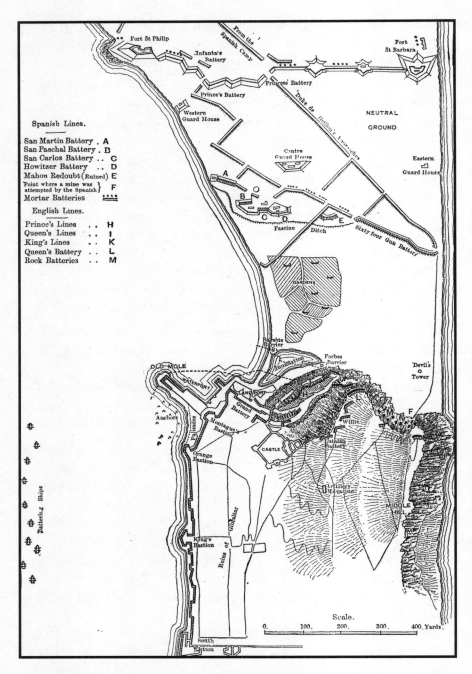

The Spanish battering ships' attack on Gibraltar, 13 September 1782.

shot that landed there. It was also noticed that some heated shot, on striking the wooden hulls, would sink in and the timber then close around the glowing cannonballs. These were left to smoulder on, inaccessible, unsuspected and unobserved by the fire-fighting parties on board. 'An incendiary bomb reached the dry part of the craft. Its effect was very slow ... the damage did not appear irremediable.'[23] An Italian officer in French service, who served on one of the battering ships, wrote afterwards:

> At two o'clock the floating battery commanded by the Prince of Nassau began to smoke on the side exposed to the garrison, and it was apprehended she had caught fire. The firing, however, continued till we could see the fortifications had taken some damage.[24]

For a long while, it seemed that neither side was gaining a significant advantage over the other, and anxious eyes on the Rock scanned the shores of the Bay for signs that the French and Spanish naval squadrons were about to join in the attack, and whether boats loaded with marines and soldiers were even at this late stage preparing to attempt an amphibious landing. John Drinkwater recalled that it might have been the intention for the Spanish gunboats and mortar-boats to join in the operation: 'About Noon, the mortar boats and bomb-ketches attempted to second the attack from the ships, but the wind having changed to the south-west, and blowing a smart breeze, with a heavy swell, they were prevented taking a part in the action.'[25] Whatever was intended, the amphibious assault did not come. De Crillon, never fully convinced of the chances for success, watched the faltering operation in mounting exasperation, and at last sent a request to Don Cordoba to bring his squadron to the close support of the floating batteries. The Admiral, who appears to have decided to have as little to do with the doomed enterprise as he could manage, sent a reply that the wind was not in his favour and he was powerless to offer assistance. In this, he was not being entirely uncooperative, as Drinkwater had already noticed the shift in the wind direction. De Crillon, however, then retired to his quarters and took very little further interest in what was going on, distancing himself as far as he was able from the unfolding failure.

The battery positions on either side of the King's Bastion shook and shivered with the repeated discharges of the heavy guns, as the British gunners gradually overwhelmed their opponents with sheer weight of metal. In the failing light of evening, the two leading battering ships were set alight from the repeated strike of heated round-shot. First, the 21-gun *Talla Piedra*'s crew had to stop their work of bombardment to attend to fires that were raging in the depths of the ship, and then those on *Pastora* did the same. Eliott's gunners concentrated their fire on that vessel and the magazine had to be flooded on orders from Don Moreno to avoid catastrophe; *Pastora* had become a helpless and impotent target. The rigging of the battering ships had been shot away early on in the attack, and they were now all immobile with some still stuck fast on the sandbanks, unless longboats could come through the storm of shot, to try to tow them away to safety. 'The most terrible thing', a Spanish officer remembered, 'was that everything failed us at once.'[26] After smoking and smouldering ominously for some time, the leading battering ships, one after another, began to burst into terrifying, unquenchable and all-consuming flames.

D'Arçon would bitterly complain that the chances for success were thrown away in undue haste:

> An order too precipitately given to wet the powder occasioned a total cessation of our cannonade ... They were all abandoned, and, as if the red-hot shot of the enemy did not do sufficient execution, the resolution was taken to set our own vessels on fire. This order was badly executed, several were absolutely set on fire before the crew had evacuated them ...[27]

The gathering night sky was now lit up with a lurid fiery scene of unspeakable horror, with the Spanish and French crews on *Pastora* and *Talla Piedra* burning to death in their separate floating infernos. The Italian officer who helped serve the guns that night wrote:

> At seven o'clock all our hopes vanished. The fire from our floating batteries entirely ceased, and rockets were thrown up as signals of distress. In short, the red-hot balls from the garrison had by this time taken such good effect, that nothing was thought of but saving the crews, and the boats of the combined fleet were immediately sent on that service. A little after midnight, the

following battery which had been the first to shows signs of conflagration, burst into flames, upon which the fire from the Rock was increased with terrific vengeance; the light produced by the flames was equal to noonday, and greatly exposed the boats of the fleet in removing the crews.[28]

Those battering ships stuck on the sandbank – *Los Dolores*, *San Christobal*, *Principe Carlos*, *Paula Secunda* and *Santa Anna* – were no longer under serious fire from the Rock, as they were irrelevant to the rest of the battle. The leading vessels, however, were being pounded to destruction. 'There was no hope of putting out the fires or of withdrawing the batteries which were stranded.'[29]

The side of the Rock and the waters of the Bay were vividly lit up with the blazing ships. Having driven off Spanish longboats, which might have been suspected of attempting a landing, the gunners on the Rock ceased bombarding the stricken vessels. They were not now a threat, and a brave effort was made to save those of the crews that could be reached. Captain Robert Curtis, whose gunboats had been engaging the Spanish ships with grape-shot from a position off the New Mole, put out to attempt a rescue. This was particularly hazardous, in the smoke and flames and the shifting shadows of that terrible night. Exploding munitions were shattering two of the ships from within, flinging burning debris and mangled bodies through the air. 'Some threw themselves into the sea, in flight from merciless fire and steel, others from drowning sought to flee by clinging to a burning keel … they burned to death amid the waves and drowned surrounded by the flames.'[30] A number of Curtis's sailors were killed and injured in the rescue attempt, but in this gallant way, over 350 Spaniards and Frenchmen were saved from the flames or from the waters of the Bay. Curtis wrote, with commendable understatement, that the scene was:

> Dreadful to a high degree. Numbers of men crying from amidst the flames, some upon pieces of wood in the water others appearing in the ships where the fire had as yet made but little progress … all imploring assistance, formed a spectacle of horror not easily to be described.[31]

A daring group of British seamen even managed to board the blazing *Pastora* and carry off the Spanish Royal Standard, which was afterwards hung from a gun in the King's Bastion. The helpless Spanish ships which had become stuck on the sandbank were soon afterwards set on fire and abandoned by their crews to avoid capture. 'Tired and fatigued, I sit down to let you know that the battle is our own,' Samuel Ancell wrote to his brother, 'we have set the enemy's ships on fire.'[32] They burned on through the night, and with the dawn their broken remnants were seen to be littering the Bay, together with scores of drowned and scorched bodies. A few wretched survivors clung to drifting debris, feebly imploring to be rescued.

The loss suffered by the Spanish and French in this futile and badly co-ordinated attack was severe, and afterwards calculated at some 1,500 killed, drowned, wounded or rescued by Curtis and his men. This figure, however, is very speculative, and other estimates put the cost at a little over 400 casualties, in addition to the 357 bedraggled prisoners pulled from the flames or out of the waters of the Bay. By stark comparison, the garrison of Gibraltar had only sixteen killed in the action (including one gunner officer, Captain Reeves), with another eighteen men wounded, and several of these casualties had been suffered during the rescue attempt of the crews of the stricken ships. The defences on the Rock had been damaged in places, it is true, but this was soon repaired. Eliott's gunners had fired 8,300 rounds, of which about half had been heated red-hot in the oven, an extraordinary effort, at almost 100 rounds fired by each gun that could be brought to bear on the battering ships.

A party of sailors and marines under Captain Gibson, RN, had set out to see if one of the stranded ships could be taken as a prize, but the fire was too far advanced and they quickly abandoned the attempt. By whichever means the battering ships had been destroyed, in practical terms it made no difference to the reality of the garrison's success. With the utter defeat of the attack, the great Spanish and French siege of Gibraltar, as an active operation with any real chance of success, was over. The report of the complete failure, carried in the *Madrid Gazette* just a week later, ran:

> When the English had made sure that the floating batteries could no longer fire, they flung into the water some of their gunboats, with which they seized several of our passing craft, thus overpowering the last remnants of troops or sailors who still remained in the batteries awaiting their turn to be rescued; so that

by this means at dawn they had taken prisoner three hundred and thirty-five persons (including various wounded, whom General Eliott is known to have treated with great humanity and kindness). The floating batteries blew up after that, with the exception of three which were completely consumed by fire.[33]

It is difficult not to feel that the whole battering-ship operation, despite the exhaustive preparations over several months, and the undeniably devoted but futile valour of their unfortunate crews, was a complete fiasco. The chances of success in attempting to subdue the gunners on the King's Bastion and neighbouring batteries with their own weight of fire was very slim in the best conditions, even assuming that the unwieldy vessels managed to get into their correct positions before beginning the attack. Had they succeeded and the British guns been forced to fall silent, little would have been achieved, as there had to be a strong and prompt follow-up, a second echelon to the attack, to build on that success. Whatever weight of fire the mortar and gunboats might have added, had they managed to get into position in good time, it seems unlikely that it would have changed the outcome very much, although Eliott's gunners would no doubt have been harder pressed.

An infantry assault, landed by sea and sent across the sands of the isthmus, had to be made, at some time and at whatever cost, if there was to be any chance of victory. There was no real plan in place for such an attempt, although Eliott claimed afterwards that 300 boats lay around the shores of the Bay ready to embark assault troops. That may have been so, but de Crillon plainly had no intention of devoting his troops to an attack when the massed British batteries had not been suppressed. The vital elements of surprise and close support were lacking almost entirely, other than from the fire of the land batteries, and it is hard to see that the lives of the Spanish and French crews were not simply thrown away, by over-confidence or neglectful inertia, or a simple lack of interest in the operation on the part of their senior officers. The Grand Attack by battering-ships on Gibraltar was no such thing, simply a flawed and ill-considered operation, with slight chance of success, carried out at the cost of the lives of hundreds of those sent into action. Eliott wrote to London with his details of the success his gunners had achieved:

On the 13th Instant at eight in the morning, all the Battering Ships commanded by Don Buenventura de Moreno, Rear-

Admiral, was put in motion and came forward to several stations previously determined they should take up, the Admiral being placed upon the Capital of the King's Bastion ... A very heavy cannonade began from all the ships, supported by Cannon and Mortars in the Enemy's Lines and Approaches; at the same instant our Batteries opened with hot and cold shot from the Guns and shells from the Howitzers and Mortars; this firing continued without intermission on both sides until noon, when that of the Enemy from the Ships seemed to slacken altho' but a little; about 2 o'clock the Admiral's Ship was observed to smoke, as if on fire ... At midnight the Admiral's Ship was plainly discovered beginning to burn ... The remaining eight ships severally blew up with violent explosions; one only escaped the effect of our fire; which it was thought proper [by the crew] to burn, there being no possibility of preserving her.[34]

The Governor ended his dispatch by adding, 'The Enemy's daring attempt by sea was effectually defeated by the constant and well supported fire from our Batteries.'

The Chevalier d'Arçon, rather inevitably, was blamed for the utter defeat of his vaunted battering ships. Whether this was due to an inherent flaw in their design, supposedly invulnerable to sustained bombardment with heated shot but plainly not so in practice, or whether the blame lay with the lack of support and co-operation from his superiors and colleagues, was hotly debated for many years. On 4 October, Robert Curtis went under a flag of truce to confer with de Crillon and arrange an exchange of prisoners (although fifty-nine refused the offer, and preferred to enlist with Eliott's garrison instead). Curtis was introduced to the Comte d'Artois, and thanked warmly for the efforts to save the men who had been trapped in the burning ships.

Good news followed hard on the success, as two weeks after the attack a Royal Navy frigate came into the Bay, with news that Admiral Earl Richard Howe, flying his flag in HMS *Victory* (100), was off Cape St Vincent and rapidly approaching the Rock with a powerful fleet. Howe had thirty-four ships-of-the-line and eight frigates and he brought with him under escort to Gibraltar a convoy of thirty-one heavily laden merchantmen. The ships had been scattered in a gale off Cape Finisterre, but were gathered together again for the final leg of the voyage past Cadiz and Cape Trafalgar, where there was most chance of interception. Howe had sent a frigate into Faro in southern Portugal on 8 October to discover from the British Consul there what was the strength of the combined Spanish and French fleet in and around the Straits of Gibraltar. Three days later, strong gale-like winds began blowing from the west, and the blockading ships in the Bay were soon in some difficulty. The Havana-built Spanish 3rd rate, *San Miguel* (74), a beautiful ship with beams of cedar and decks of mahogany, ran aground in the gale near the Ragged Staff Wharf, and was boarded and seized by the troops of the garrison, together with her crew of 650 men. She was re-floated and moored at the New Mole. Although the Spaniards bombarded the warship to try to prevent the repairs, the work was carried out successfully, and this fine nine-year-old vessel was eventually taken into the service of the Royal Navy, refitted and renamed HMS *Saint Michael*, under the command of Sir Charles Knowles.

The strong westerlies drove Howe's warships and the convoy past the Rock, and into the Mediterranean. The Admiral had some difficulty gathering his vulnerable charges together again to beat back towards harbour, although the frigate *Latona* (34) managed to get in first time, with four merchantmen whose commanders, either through chance or good management, did not overshoot the entrance to the Bay. Don Cordoba's own ships had been riding at single anchor, ready to move out to engage Howe, and had suffered some damage in the gale which had driven *San Miguel* ashore. However, on 13 October the Admiral took advantage of a change in the wind to put out from the Bay to try to split Howe's escorts away from the merchantmen. This he failed to do, even though he could deploy forty-six ships, and the British captains now had to contend with the current flowing in through the Straits, as they made their way into Gibraltar. However, the wind again changed for the better, and the remaining transports all came safely into harbour in straggling fashion by 17 October, 'standing under easy sail', guarded and watched over by the escorting warships. Howe was impatient to get back into the open sea, and he wrote of the successful operation: 'On the 17th the rest of the store-ships were likewise anchored in Rosia Bay. I proposed to take advantage immediately of the easterly wind for returning through the Strait to the westward.'[35]

The third relief of the garrison had been accomplished in fine style with a neat piece of seamanship, almost literally while the blockaders and besiegers looked on. Howe had manoeuvred his squadron to shield the transports as they made their way into the Bay, but he was wary of bringing on a general action with his more numerous opponents. The main task had been to resupply the garrison on the Rock and this was achieved after something of a scramble in the strong winds, and Howe's purpose was now not to engage in one-sided naval actions, but to get his fleet back to the English Channel. The Admiral wrote:

> At break of day on the 19th the combined force of the enemy was seen at a little distance to the north-east. The British fleet being at that time so nearly between Europa and Ceuta Points, there was not space to form in order of battle on either tack, I therefore re-passed the Straits, followed by the enemy.[36]

This may have been a matter of necessity, but observers on the Rock watched in some dismay as Howe was apparently pursued by Don Cordoba through the Straits, as if in flight, on the way back to England. John Drinkwater wrote, 'Though fully convinced of the prudence of His Lordship's conduct, it was no very pleasing prospect for a British garrison to behold a British fleet, though inferior in force, lead the enemy.'[37] The captain did not seem to be very convinced, but he was, of course, in no position to judge Howe's actions right or wrong.

Having gained sea-room in which to manoeuvre properly, Howe slackened his pace, so that at sunrise on 20 October, the opposing fleets sighted each other about eighteen miles off Cape Spartel on the Barbary coast. By 1pm both admirals had formed their ships into line of battle, although Howe's captains showed a frustrating inability to conform promptly to his signals (a number of which had been recently introduced and so were unfamiliar). The huge Havana-built 120-gun Spanish flagship, *Santisima Trinidad*, gradually drew opposite the centre of Howe's line, opposed by HMS *Victory* and *Prince Royal* (98). Firing began at 6pm between Don Cordoba's van and Howe's rear division, eleven ships-of-the-line commanded by Rear Admiral Sir Richard Hughes on *Princess Amelia* (84). Vice Admiral Millbank, aboard the *Ocean* (90), wrote in his report:

> A very superior force meditated the design of cutting off our rear, in which they would probably have succeeded, had we not preserved a very close line. The attack was made by a vice-

Admiral bearing Spanish colours, seconded by a French Commodore, two three-deckers, and thirteen sail of the line ... I have great reason to judge that those, who did engage us, met with a very severe reception.[38]

The sound of the guns could be clearly heard on the Rock, but the opposing squadrons were now out of sight. When darkness fell, little serious damage had been inflicted by either side, although some 639 casualties had been suffered between the contending fleets, distributed in broadly equal proportions. At the following dawn, Don Cordoba found that, although he had the weather gauge, Howe's swifter ships, with their coppered hulls, had drawn eight miles ahead and were not to be caught. The Spanish naval commander would claim to have driven Howe off, but this was very suspect, as Don Cordoba had proved quite incapable of preventing the resupply of Eliott's garrison, despite having a greater number of ships at sea.

In addition to the stores, matériel, 1,500 barrels of powder and round-shot landed, were the 1,600 men of the 25th Regiment of Foot and the 59th Foot, although the brig *Minerva*, carrying their wives and families and the regimental stocks of clothing, was seized by the Spaniards after losing her masts in the gale. These unfortunates were not released from internment until the end of the year, when the bedraggled party was sent to Gibraltar; the soldiers' clothing was not returned, of course, and the two regiments were ill-clad for the rest of the siege and presented a sorry sight, much to Eliott's irritation. 'A flag of truce', John Drinkwater wrote, 'on the 20th, had informed us that the women belonging to the 25th and 59th Regiments were at the enemy's camp, waiting more moderate weather to be sent by water into the garrison. The 22nd they were received, but upon their landing, they were conducted to the Naval hospital.'[39] The unfortunate fact was that a number of the women were suspected of suffering from venereal disease, and Eliott was concerned at the likely impact of their arrival upon his soldiers.

Howe got back to Spithead on 14 November, having detached Rear Admiral Hughes with six warships to the West Indies. The Admiral found that he was criticized for avoiding a full action against the Spanish and French fleet, but he had accomplished his objective, the resupply of the Gibraltar garrison. There had been no reason to risk an unequal battle, when his own judgement was plainly that the odds against success were too long. Any serious damage to his ships could not readily be repaired, unlike those of his opponents, who were fortunate to have many friendly ports close at hand. The Admiral was satisfied with what he had achieved: 'A more essential piece of naval service to this country was never performed.'[40] Against this was the widely believed rumour that several of the transports had not been fully unloaded in Gibraltar harbour, as their captains were disappointed at the low prices their goods would command, and preferred to take them elsewhere as soon as the opportunity arose.

With Howe's relief of Gibraltar, so soon after the defeat of the battering ships, it was plain to most commanders – British, Hanoverian, Spanish and French – that the siege was now all but over, with no real prospect of success for Madrid and Paris. Still, on the night of 23 October the gunboats attacked again, and sank the cutter *Hector*, with all her crew being drowned. Despite this, activity steadily diminished, and it was noticed that troops were leaving the camp near San Roques and the Orange Grove in substantial numbers, and marching away with bands playing bravely, as if from some field of victory. Firing from the batteries continued each day, as if neither side could bear to break the routine, and the dismal tally of casualties went on. Gibraltar Bay saw some sharp little actions between opposing gunboats, as can be seen from a letter written by Governor Eliott on 19 December: 'Captain Gibson led a squadron of eight Gun-boats against the enemy's thirty in all, he went out at least a mile with the wind at East and fairly drove the Spaniards in, kicking 'em all the way.' A week later he commented, 'Gun and Mortar Boats now come in the day, lie at a great distance and little Gibson leads his squadron to meet them.'[41]

These activities seemed to have little purpose now, and monotony became the daily norm once again, with a noticeable lowering of discipline. 'Wine being in plenty,' John Spilsbury remembered, 'the soldiers now lead a very disorderly life, and are constantly quarrelling.'[42] It was not just the junior ranks that became involved in the renewed disorder, 'Some officers have been engaged in a riot against some Sergeants of the 73rd at a dance, and some others in breaking open a ward in the hospital and attacking the women there.'[43] All this seemed to indicate a growing lack of purpose, with apparently little to fear from the besieging forces, with months and long years of tedious blockade and siege stretching behind the garrison. However, Eliott had the men begin to repair the battered defences, to occupy their spare time usefully, and as a precaution against any suddenly renewed attack, however unlikely this now seemed. 'The enemy's cannonade from the land, except when the gun-boats fired, was at this time so trifling that it scarcely deserved the name,' Drinkwater remembered. 'Our engineers were therefore employed in repairing the curtain of the Grand Battery, the North Face and the flank of Montague's Bastion … though the men were much exposed in this duty, the enemy seldom if ever molested them.'[44]

That Proud Fortress

The Convention of Aranjuez, agreed in 1779, had firmly bound France to assist Spain in the attempt to recover Gibraltar. King Carlos III still had hopes that, even now, a grand assault might carry the defences on the Rock, although the failure of the battering ships' attack, and the third relief under Admiral Howe, had badly dented that aspiration. The French field commander at the siege, the Duc de Crillon, was not at all interested in making another such attempt, which would just have wasted the lives of many of his soldiers with little prospect of success. It seemed quite clear that the garrison could not be overwhelmed by military or naval force. Following the capitulation of the British army under Lord Cornwallis at Yorktown in Virginia in October 1781, the war in North America had slowly shuffled towards an untidy end. George III's new Prime Minister, Lord Shelburne, was anxious for peace, which, courtesy of Rodney's naval victory at the Saintes, might now be had on better terms than otherwise would be on offer. The government in London felt obliged to express an intention to continue the conflict, but money, political will and public support to go on was lacking; the preliminary peace agreement with the Americans was signed on 30 November 1782.

There were renewed discussions in London over whether Gibraltar, even after so much effort, treasure and blood had been devoted to its defence, should yet be returned to Spanish occupancy and rule. 'I think peace in every way necessary to this country,' George III wrote, 'and I shall not think it complete if we do not get rid of Gibraltar.'[1] If Minorca could be had in exchange, perhaps together with Florida (where the British garrison in Pensacola had been besieged by Spanish troops), and certain islands in the West Indies, then so much the better, and interest in such an arrangement was certainly genuine in London. Nothing came of this notion – British public opinion, fired by Eliott's fine defence of the Rock, would be outraged, while Carlos III would not consider giving up key islands in the Caribbean, and the whole notion was quietly dropped.

France had obtained its principal objective in the war, with the newly independent American colonies presumably dutifully grateful to Paris, and British influence diminished, although no fresh foothold in Canada had been achieved. Louis XVI's Foreign Minister, the Comte de Vergennes, suggested to Don Arenda, the Spanish Ambassador in Paris, that if Spain would cease its attempt to take Gibraltar by force, Great Britain could be persuaded to relinquish any claim to Minorca, and allow Madrid a free hand in East Florida. Don Arenda, perhaps having more regard to French interests in ensuring that the British gave up Minorca for good, than to the stated preferences of his own King for the claim to recover the Rock to be pursued, promptly agreed to this arrangement. Carlos III wrote ruefully to Louis XVI on 2 January 1783: 'My Ambassador, knowing my heart's tender sentiments for You, has allowed himself to exceed my orders and pursue peace negotiations without insisting on the cession of Gibraltar.'[2] Spain had still hoped to recover the place by negotiation, and Don Arenda's ready acceptance of the proposed terms had over-stepped his authority, allowing France an excuse to withdraw from a war that was no longer worth fighting. However, the Spanish King was employing his memory rather selectively and did Don Arenda less than justice. Confidential instructions had been sent that the claim to the Rock could be bargained away, if necessary. Prime Minister Floridablanca wrote at the time, 'The only difficulty in the way of peace is Gibraltar ... The King wishes to support this compromise with all his might.'[3] A few years later he would write, 'We must get it back whenever we can, either by negotiation or by force. We have given way on Gibraltar only for the moment.'[4] Expediency and national interest were apparently dishes that could be taken or set aside at will, depending on circumstances.

For good or ill, the preliminary Articles to cease hostilities were signed on 20 January 1783, and the long-held hope of regaining Gibraltar, however faint that might have been after the disappointments of more than three years of unsuccessful blockade and siege, was the price paid by Madrid so that Paris could have peace. The formal Treaty of Versailles would eventually be concluded on 3 September, and Spain had managed, almost against the run of play, to enlarge its possessions in the Caribbean and Florida and had regained Minorca, an undoubted prize. Still, once again, Gibraltar was not explicitly mentioned and so its status remained as at the Treaty of Utrecht in 1713. Feelings were undoubtedly still mixed in London over what was being signed away, as George III commented rather wistfully, 'I should have liked Minorca, and the two Floridas [East and West] and Guadeloupe better than that proud fortress, and in my opinion source of another war, or at least of a constant lurking enmity.'[5]

On 2 February 1783 the Spanish crew in the afternoon truce-boat, which each day exchanged selected mail with the garrison, called out that hostilities were over, and that Spain and Great Britain were friends once more: 'Todos Amigos.' Firing was suspended and Samuel Ancell noted, 'Would you believe that last night every post appeared solitary, by the silence which everywhere prevailed, and the hours of slumber seemed uneasy.'[6] Eliott remained understandably cautious, but three days later he received formal news from the Duc de Crillon that the peace preliminaries had indeed been signed between Great Britain, Spain and France. The blockade and siege of Gibraltar were declared to be at an end and the port was once again open, although the garrison on the Rock took the opportunity, rather ungraciously, to fire one last shot over the Spanish trenches for good measure. Perhaps it was a negligent discharge and not maliciously intended. On 5 March, a schooner put into Gibraltar harbour with a present of bullocks from the Sultan of Morocco. The captain of the vessel also carried a letter to Eliott from the Sultan, expressing warm congratulations on his success in resisting the siege, adding rather mendaciously that prayers had been said for the defeat of the battering ships' attack. The schooner also carried a party of twenty-six Corsican volunteers who had been seized 'by mistake' on their way to join the garrison, and were now sent on their way. Not everyone greeted the news of peace with acclaim, as the lack of success by the besiegers was very evident, and one Spanish naval officer wrote at the time, 'I have never heard so much news of peace as in these days ... It is good for the nation, but for those who make their careers by the sword, it is not good.'[7]

The frigate HMS *Thetis*, commanded by Captain Blackell, put into Gibraltar Bay on 10 March with dispatches from England. These contained confirmation that the peace preliminaries had indeed been concluded. The gates of Gibraltar were unlocked two days later with solemn ceremony, and Eliott and de Crillon met for the first time; the commanders greeted each other with elaborate courtesy at a point midway between the Bayside Barrier and the forward Spanish entrenchments. Dismounting, the two men stood in easy conversation for a few moments, before Eliott and his staff officers were taken to see the Spanish entrenchments and fortifications. They were also shown a mine that the Spanish engineers had begun to dig under the Devil's Tower, but they had not had time to take the work very far, although the garrison had heard the detonations as they tried to make their way forward. The whole party then went to supper with de Crillon and his senior officers in San Roques, before they returned to Gibraltar, after exchanging salutes and expressions of mutual esteem and respect with their solicitous hosts.

De Crillon returned the compliment by paying a formal visit to Gibraltar on 31 March, accompanied by a large party of officers, including the elderly Marquis de Saya (a remarkable veteran of the siege in 1727), Comte de Jamaigne and Comte de Serano. All were understandably eager to see the defences on the Rock, and were taken on a tour of the fortifications that had defied their best efforts for so long. They were appropriately impressed, expressing particular admiration at Ince's tunnelling works. De Crillon took the trouble to quietly assure his hosts that the fatally flawed battering ships' attack had been none of his doing. He was slightly embarrassed by the punctilious salutes that he received everywhere he went, as each regiment that he rode past turned out to present arms and salute him with three hearty, but slightly mocking, cheers. The Marquis entered into the spirit of the occasion and acknowledged the salutes by doffing his hat and bowing slightly towards the cheering soldiers. After being entertained to a dinner by Eliott and the senior officers of the garrison, he departed for his own camp with his aides, commenting rather ruefully to some gunner officers, 'I would rather see you here as friends … you never spared me.'[8] De Crillon was then nearly thrown from his horse when a gun, part of a salute fired in his honour, frightened the animal; luckily, he suffered no real hurt other than slightly bruised dignity.

A few days later, the Duc de Crillon went off to Madrid, where he appeared to neatly avoid serious censure over the failure to take the Rock. He was succeeded in command on the ground by the elderly Marquis de Saya, who had the rather unglamorous task to oversee the demolition of the forward Spanish entrenchments on the isthmus, and to take down the huge camp that had grown up at the foot of the Queen of Spain's Chair. Having served as a junior officer in the siege of 1727, de Saya was well acquainted with the area. 'The return of tranquility,' Captain John

Drinkwater wrote, 'this prospect of plenty, and relief from the daily vexations could not fail to diffuse a general joy throughout the Garrison.'[9] However, it was some months before the Spanish troops fully withdrew behind their original lines across the neck of the isthmus, causing Eliott to complain to de Saya several times before he complied. There were also continued trivial and mean interruptions to mail coming to and from Gibraltar, and fishermen once more setting out from the Rock were harassed by Spanish gunboats.

So came to an end the longest continuous formal siege in history; at a cost to the garrison of 333 killed, 536 dead of sickness and disease, 1,191 wounded and injured, and 43 deserters, the Rock had been held for Great Britain. Of the 485 Royal Artillery gunners involved, no fewer than 196 had been killed, a tellingly high percentage, far exceeding that of any other individual unit. Civilian casualties were not recorded, but were not insignificant, and there is no certain figure for the undoubtedly heavier losses suffered by the Spanish and French besiegers.

The expenditure of artillery munitions during the Great Siege was quite extraordinary. Between September 1779 and February 1783, Eliott's gunners fired 57,163 round-shot of all calibres, 129,151 mortars bombs, 12,681 grape-shot rounds, 926 inflammable 'carcasses', and 679 illuminating light balls. Such astonishing exactness should, of course, be treated with some caution, while Mercier's novel air-burst shells seem not to be listed as an item. Over 8,000 barrels of powder had been used up by the garrison, while the British naval ships and gunboats operating in Gibraltar Bay fired more than 4,700 round-shot. In reply, the Spanish and French gunners, who could hardly be accused of failing to do their best under trying circumstances, fired an estimated 244,104 rounds of all types at the Rock from their land batteries, with another 14,283 from gunboats and battering ships.[10] Once again, the figures are remarkably and surprisingly exact, but they give a truly astonishing total of almost half a million rounds exchanged by the opposing sides during the course of the prolonged siege operations. To these figures may be added the expenditure in ordnance by Rodney's, Darby's and Howe's crews while engaged with their Spanish and French opponents on the high seas. From start to finish, the campaign on land and afloat had largely been a gunnery affair.

This British success guaranteed for the cruising squadrons of the Royal Navy free access into the Mediterranean, with the sheltered anchorage at

Gibraltar now so much more important after the loss of Minorca (although the British would briefly re-occupy that island during the French Revolutionary War). The successful conclusion to the operations, against what had appeared to be overwhelming odds, was greeted with great rejoicing in Great Britain. Not only had Gibraltar been held, but Eliott's defence of the place had tied down large numbers of Spanish and, to a lesser extent, French, military and naval forces in an ultimately fruitless campaign. These might have been used to greater effect elsewhere, particularly against the valuable British island possessions in the West Indies. The same argument may be made about the diversion of British effort which might have been employed in holding on to the American colonies, or protecting Great Britain's merchant fleet, which suffered heavily at the hands of the French, Dutch and Spanish navies and from the depredations of American privateers. Nevertheless this was a resounding military victory, at a time when victories were in lamentably short supply. Both Houses of Parliament passed votes of thanks to Eliott for his efforts, together with the grant of a pension. King George III conferred on him the Order of the Bath, and the Governor was invested with the insignia of the Order by Robert Boyd, acting as His Majesty's representative for the occasion, at a grand parade on the King's Bastion, held on St George's Day, 23 April 1783, while a military band rendered that sprightly air, 'See the Conquering Hero Come'.

'No army', Eliott told his assembled soldiers in his congratulatory address on their success,

> has ever been rewarded by higher national honours, and it is well known how great, universal, and spontaneous were the rejoicings throughout the kingdom, upon the news of your success ... I now most warmly congratulate you on these united and brilliant testimonies of approbation, amidst such numerous, such exalted, tokens of applause; and forgive me, faithful companions, if I humbly crave your acceptance of my grateful acknowledgements.'[11]

After the parade was dismissed, the soldiers were treated to a celebratory meal of a pound of fresh beef and a quart of good wine each. Governor Eliott and his staff, and the senior officers of the garrison, enjoyed a pleasant supper at the convent in the Town, while fireworks, fired from the King's Bastion, illuminated the night sky over the Bay.

With the arrival of peace, the garrison would naturally be reduced from a war establishment, and all but the recently arrived and freshly re-equipped 25th Foot and the 59th Foot, were soon sent home. They would be replaced with fresh regiments, including the 11th Foot and the 32nd Foot, who had been stationed in Ireland. Eliott had calculated that 4,000 men would be required as a minimum for the garrison in peacetime, both to maintain the security of the place, and also to rebuild and restore the now rather battered defences, after long years of Spanish and French bombardment, when little other than emergency repairs could be undertaken. To maintain the strength of the regiments that were to remain, generous bounties of one and a half guineas each were offered to time-expired soldiers to re-enlist, and many did so, some 800 men prolonging their stay within the confines of the Rock in this way. The veteran regiments had all embarked for Great Britain by the end of October 1783, some to be disbanded as no longer required for peace-time service. Among these was John Drinkwater's 72nd Regiment of Foot, the short-lived Royal Manchester Volunteers, who were treated to a lavish banquet by the civic dignitaries of that city on 7 September, when their Colours were laid up. The 2/73rd Foot was also disbanded, but many of the officers took up an offer to transfer to the 1/73rd, then serving in India. The Corsican volunteers were paid off, thanked for their services, and given passage to any convenient port of their choice.

Eliott also had the agreeable task of arranging the distribution of the considerable prize monies awarded during the siege. These sums were vast by the values of the day and included £16,000 for the battering ships, and £14,000 for the captured *San Miguel*, now serving with the Royal Navy as HMS *Saint Michael*. As commander of the garrison, the Governor quite naturally received the largest share, prize money of £3,375 together with his pension of £1,500 per annum (Robert Boyd received £937). Eliott remained on the Rock as Governor for four years following the end of the siege, supervising the rebuilding works, keeping a careful eye on what the Spanish were doing (noting that they were slow to demolish their works across the isthmus, as was required under the terms of the peace treaty), and working to restore good relations with the Sultan of Morocco. Although increasingly frail, deaf and short-tempered, he was also active on behalf of the welfare of the time-expired veterans of the Great Siege, particularly those who had been incapacitated by injury or wounds. He sought a special pension for

Thomas Chisholme, the surgeon of the 56th Foot, who had lost his right leg and had the other broken by the same Spanish round-shot. Eliott was asked to recommend twenty sergeants for admission to the Royal Hospital, Chelsea, at an additional pension of one shilling a day. 'No men', he wrote warmly, 'could be more worthy such provision from their country.'[12]

On his return to Great Britain in 1787, George Augustus Eliott was at last raised to the peerage as 1st Baron Heathfield of Gibraltar, taking the name from the elegant estate in Sussex that he had purchased with the prize money awarded to him after the capture of Havana in 1762. He was preparing to return and take up his duties in Gibraltar once more, but died in Aachen in northern Germany on 6 July 1790, where he had gone to take the waters for his declining health. Four years later his second-in-command during the siege, 84-year-old Robert Boyd also died, while serving as Eliott's successor as Governor of the Rock; he had also been awarded the Order of the Bath, although his efforts were, inevitably, rather eclipsed by those of Eliott. Boyd was buried in the King's Bastion, as he had wished, the formidable defensive work that he ordered to be begun in 1775, and which had stood the garrison in such good stead during the long months of the siege.

The Great Siege of Gibraltar, three years, seven months and five days long, for all the inadequacies and imperfections of the Spanish and French operations, had been a severe test of nerve and will, and of military steadfastness, at a time of uncertainty for Great Britain. The discipline and good order of the garrison had, at times, been in doubt, but their steadfastness under attack had not. Charles James Fox, the great parliamentary orator, put the feeling in London rather well, when addressing the House of Commons shortly before the end of the operations:

> The fortress of Gibraltar was to be reckoned amongst the most valuable possessions of England. It was that which gave us respect in the eyes of nations; it manifested our superiority and gave us the means of obliging them by protection. Give up to Spain the fortress of Gibraltar, and the Mediterranean becomes to them a pond on which they can navigate at pleasure, and act without control or check. Deprive yourselves of this station and the States of Europe who border on the Mediterranean will no

longer look to you for the free navigation of that sea, and having it no longer in your power to be useful, you cannot expect alliances.[13]

To hold the Rock for so long, in the face of daunting odds, had been an epic military endeavour, arguably the most formidable such operation to take place in the entire eighteenth century, and it was one of the most remarkable of all such operations. At the same time, it could not be denied that the blockade and siege itself lacked co-ordination and failed to bite. 'The use that was made of the combined fleets of France and Spain could not have been less skilful or more incomprehensible ... they did not prevent the arrival of large convoys or play an important part in the principal bombardments.'[14] Despite this, the British achievement was widely recognized at the time as a memorable triumph. This remains so, unmarred by the fact that Great Britain several times, before, during, and after the siege, tried to negotiate possession of the Rock away if more favourable military bases and trading terms could be secured elsewhere.

No less than for Spain and France, the major British naval efforts to sustain Eliott's garrison in Gibraltar proved to be a serious distraction from the troubled task of winning the war for the North American colonies. Had the Royal Navy been free to devote its full strength to operations on the Atlantic seaboard, cutting off the vital French support for the American rebels, at a time when their efforts were flagging, the War of Independence might well have proved to be no such thing. As it was, the American colonies slipped away and, arguably, this was the price that was paid for Great Britain's continued possession of the Rock.

Gibraltar was never again so closely or energetically besieged. The valuable sheltered anchorage received the battered ships after Lord Nelson's victory at Trafalgar in October 1805, and the naval base and facilities were greatly extended and improved throughout the nineteenth century. With the introduction of rifled artillery, whose long reach enabled the gunners on the Rock to command the Straits of Gibraltar properly, also came the ability of rifled batteries situated on the Spanish mainland to have made Gibraltar untenable. The use of offensive air-power from the 1920s onwards would have had the same effect in no time at all, but this was never put to the test, although Spain remained unreconciled to the loss of the territory, and has ever longed for its return.

The soldiers of Eliott's garrison, quite justly proud of their achievement, dispersed to pursue their careers and fortunes on other fields of war, or were retired as invalids or pensioners, recounting their stirring exploits to children and grandchildren as time went on. A veteran of the Great Siege, Private Gordon of the 73rd Foot, wrote, 'A common soldier, although he has an equal share of danger ... is far from having an equal share of glory; yet, I know not how it is, I have a desire, and I believe everyone has the same, that it should be known I was at Gibraltar, and fought and conquered.'[15]

The Cock of the Rock
General Sir George Eliott, 1st Baron Heathfield of Gibraltar

George Augustus Eliott, 1st Baron Heathfield (1717–90), was born on Christmas Day in Scotland, the seventh and youngest son of Sir Gilbert Eliott, Baronet, of Stobs. The young man was educated at Leiden University in the Netherlands, and at the French military college of La Fère, which had been founded by the famed military engineer, Marshal Vauban. After service as a volunteer with the Prussian Army during 1735 and 1736, he returned to study at the Royal Military Academy at Woolwich, and in 1739 was commissioned into the 2nd Squadron of the Horse Grenadier Guards, and simultaneously held a commission as an engineer officer, as there was no regular corps of sappers and miners at that time. He served through the War of Austrian Succession (1742–48), being wounded at Dettingen (1743), and was present at Fontenoy (1745). Between 1756 and 1759 Eliott was an aide-de-camp to King George II, and in 1759 he raised the 1st Light Horse (15th Light Dragoons/Hussars). He fought at Minden that year, in command of a brigade of cavalry, being then promoted to Major General, and taking a prominent part in the cavalry charge at Emsdorf in 1760, for which George II accorded his regiment the 'Royal' title. In 1763 Eliott took part in the expedition to Havana, as second-in-command to the Earl of Albemarle, and became Lieutenant General in 1765 (backdated to 1761). Made wealthy by the award of over £25,000 of prize money from the successful expedition, and an advantageous marriage to an heiress, Eliott bought an elegant estate at Heathfield in Sussex.

Between 1774 and 1775 Eliott was commander-in-chief in Ireland, but he disliked the restrictions that petty political infighting in Dublin imposed on the role, and soon sought replacement. This was done, and he was appointed Governor of Gibraltar, arriving on the Rock on board

HMS *Worcester* on 25 May 1777. The following year he was made General, and in 1779 the siege of the Rock by the Spaniards and French began. On 8 January 1783, Eliott received the thanks of Parliament for his services at the siege, and was made a Knight of the Bath on 6 February that year, being invested with that honour at Gibraltar on 23 April. In May 1787 he returned to England, and was created Lord Heathfield (1st Baron Heathfield of Gibraltar) on 14 June. Although increasingly dogged by age and infirmity, Eliott still held the post of Governor of Gibraltar, and in 1790 was making his way back to the Rock when he was taken ill at Aachen in Germany, apparently after drinking a surfeit of mineral water. Eliott suffered a severe stroke, and died on 6 July. Brought back to England, George Eliott was buried at Heathfield Churchyard in Sussex. The descriptive name-plate on the coffin was made from metal recovered from one of the sunken battering ships lying in the Bay of Gibraltar.

A dedicated professional soldier, George Augustus Eliott was a rather dour man, abstemious, a non-drinker and vegetarian by habit. He was nonetheless energetic and hard-working, with a certain dry sense of humour and genuinely interested in the capabilities and welfare of his troops. He took constant care to improve both his own military knowledge and that of his officers and men. As a young man he had gained a good reputation as a skilled leader of light cavalry, but was equally adept at the complex technology of positional siege warfare. His indomitable and uncompromising nature, as when refusing to permit the inoculation against smallpox at the height of the Siege of Gibraltar, was noticeable, and he was perhaps respected and admired rather than liked. Eliott's resilience and resourcefulness in the most arduous circumstances of the long, uncertain months of the Great Siege of Gibraltar certainly attracted wide admiration, both in Great Britain and across Europe, in what was rightly regarded as one of the epic military operations of the eighteenth century. At the time, he was seen as a true British Hero, and it is easy to see why this was so.

Incidentally, the soubriquet 'Cock of the Rock' was also accorded to a later Governor, Charles O'Hara, who reputedly kept two mistresses in different quarters of the Old Town, at the same time.

The Opposing Land Forces in the Great Siege

The Gibraltar Garrison

21 June 1779, at the commencement of the Spanish blockade

Governor	General Sir George Augustus Eliott
Deputy Governor	Lieutenant General Sir Robert Boyd
Commander of the Hanoverian Brigade	Major General De la Motte
Chief of Artillery	Colonel John Godwin

Artillerymen	485	
Chief of Engineers		Lieutenant Colonel William Green
Engineers and Soldier–Artificers	122	
12th Regiment of Foot	599	Lieutenant Colonel Thomas Trigge
39th Regiment of Foot	586	Colonel Charles Ross
56th Regiment of Foot	587	Major Bulleine Fancourt
58th Regiment of Foot	605	Lieutenant Colonel Gavin Cochrane
72nd Regiment of Foot (the Royal Manchester Volunteers)	1,046	Lieutenant Colonel George Gledstanes
Hardenberg's Regiment	452	Lieutenant Colonel Hugo
Reden's Regiment	444	Lieutenant Colonel Dachenhausen
De la Motte's Regiment	456	Lieutenant Colonel Schlippergill
Total	5,382*	

*In addition to the 'Marine Brigade', 760 naval officers and seamen serving ashore in 1782–3.

Landed January 1780		
2/73rd Regiment of Foot (McLeod's Highlanders)	1,052	Lieutenant Colonel George McKenzie

Landed March 1782		
97th Regiment of Foot	700	Lieutenant Colonel Samuel Stanton
Landed October 1782		
25th Regiment of Foot	800	
59th Regiment of Foot	800	

The Royal Navy squadron in Gibraltar at the time of the commencement of the Great Siege comprised:

HMS *Panther* (60)
HMS *Enterprise* (28)
HMS *Childers* (14)
HMS *Gibraltar* (12)
HMS *Fortune* (10)

The Spanish–French Besieging Force

13–14 September 1782 (at the time of the battering ships' attack)

(Recorded by Captain John Drinkwater in his account of the Great Siege)

Spanish Infantry Units

Unit	No. of battalions	Strength
Gardes Espagnoles	4	3,033
Gardes Wallones	4	3,027
Saboya Regiment	1	720
Cordova Regiment	1	719
Burgos Regiment	2	1,440
Murcia Regiment	2	1,440
Ultonia Regiment	1	721
Volunteers of Aragon	1	405
1st Regiment of Catalonia	2	1,850
La Princessa Regiment	1	729
Naples Regiment	2	1,440
Betchart Regiment	2	1,234
Grenadiers	2	1,374
Provincial Grenadiers	6	4,710
Dismounted Dragoons	2	2,440
Artillerymen and Engineers		1,341

Spanish Cavalry Units

Unit	No. of squadrons
Regiment de Farnese	1
Regiment d'Alcantara	1
Regiment d'Algarves	1
Regiment de Calatrava	1
Regiment de San Iago	1
Regiment de Mendoza	1
Regiment de Volontaires	1
Regiment de Lusitania	2
Dragoons de Pavie	2

French Infantry Units

Unit	No. of battalions	Strength
Régiment de Lyonnais	1	1,085
Régiment de Bouillon	1	1,073
Régiment de Bretagne	1	1,077
Royal Suédois Regiment	1	1,061 (German recruited)
Artillerymen and Engineers	not known	

French Cavalry Units

Unit	No. of squadrons
Régiment de Roi	1
Régiment de la Reine	1
Régiment du Prince	1
Régiment de Bourbon	2

Total Spanish and French strength estimated at 33,000 all ranks.

Appendix 3

The Gibraltar Battle Honours

The British regiments that were awarded the 'Gibraltar' battle honour were:

12th Regiment of Foot (Suffolks/Royal Anglian Regiment)

39th Regiment of Foot (Dorsets/Devonshire & Dorset Light Infantry/The Rifles). Note: the 39th was the only regiment to take part in the defence of the Rock in 1713 (as Newton's), in 1726–28 (as Sankey's), and during 1779–83.

56th Regiment of Foot (Essex/Royal Anglian Regiment)

58th Regiment of Foot (Northamptonshire/Royal Anglian Regiment)

73rd Regiment of Foot (71st/Highland Light Infantry/Royal Highland Fusiliers/Royal Regiment of Scotland)

19/5 (Gibraltar 1779–83) Battery, Royal Artillery

23 (Gibraltar 1779–83) Commando Headquarters Battery, Royal Artillery.

(The 72nd Regiment of Foot, the Royal Manchester Volunteers, and the 97th Regiment of Foot, were both disbanded at the cessation of hostilities. Neither the 25th Regiment of Foot nor the 59th Regiment of Foot were awarded the battle honour, as they arrived on the Rock relatively late in the siege.)

The Gibraltar Cuff-Title Band

'Mit Eliot zu Ruhm und Sieg'[1]

The Hanoverian Regiments of von Reden, De la Motte and von Hardenberg were sent to Gibraltar as a part of the garrison in October 1775, releasing time-expired troops to go home, and other British units for service in the rebellious American colonies. The Hanoverian soldiers served throughout the Great Siege, and had a good reputation for discipline. They were afterwards permitted by King George III the honour of wearing a blue cloth cuff title, embroidered GIBRALTAR, on the lower right sleeve of their tunic, the waffenrock.

When Hanover was incorporated into Prussia, after the war in 1866, the three regiments were renamed Fusilier Regiment General Feldmarschall Prinz Albrecht von Preussen (Hannoversches) Nr 73, Regiment Von Voigts-Rhetz (3 Hannoversches) Nr 79, and Hannoversches Jäger Battalion Nr 10. The newly renamed units retained the GIBRALTAR cuff-band honour – all of yellow lettering embroidered on blue of varying shades. It seems that all ranks wore the embroidered version of a standard quality, although there is some evidence that a gold-wire embroidered version for officers' use was authorized at one time.

The cuff-bands were further authorized for wear in January 1901 by Kaiser Wilhelm II, and during the Great War these continued in use. 'We were known as "Les Gibraltars" on account of the blue Gibraltar colours we wore in memory.'[2] *The Illustrated War News*, published in London in August 1917, featured an article which showed two rather forlorn-looking steel-helmeted German officers, who had been taken prisoner and were waiting to be questioned by their British captors. The officer standing closest to the photographer is clearly wearing the GIBRALTAR cuff-band.

Notes

Introduction: Noble Impartiality and Impatient Ambition

1. 'Spain lost a limb in Gibraltar … They could not bear an English Garrison in their Country without every effort to remove them.' Plá, J, *Gibraltar*, 1955, p. 50. Without entering into an argument over who was in the right on this vexatious subject, it is worth remembering that Gibraltar was a Spanish possession for a shorter time than it has since been in British hands (with no very evident desire amongst present-day Gibraltarians to change their allegiance).
2. B Cornwell, *A Description of Gibraltar, with an Account of the Blockade*, 1782, p. 47.
3. E Bradford, *Gibraltar, the History of a Fortress*, 1971, p. 39.
4. J Russell, *Gibraltar Besieged, 1779-1783*, 1965, p. 259.
5. F Sayer, *The History of Gibraltar*, 1865, pp. 286–7.
6. J Muller, *The Attac and Defence of Fortified Places*, 1757, p. 1 (note: 'Attac' is correct).
7. J Grant, *British Battles on Land and Sea*, 1880, p. 178.

Chapter 1: A Little World of Itself

1. J Drinkwater, *A History of the Late Siege of Gibraltar* (1785), pp. 1 and 51. The Berber chief, Tariq ibn Zayyad, captured the Rock from the Christian King Roderic of the Goths in 711.
2. B Cornwell, *A Description of Gibraltar, with an Account of the Blockade* (1782), p. 47.
3. E Bradford, *Gibraltar: The History of a Fortress* (1971), p. 43.
4. Ibid., p. 46.
5. J Plá, *Gibraltar* (1955), p. 30.
6. Ibid.
7. J Falkner, *Marlborough's Wars* (2005), p. 213.
8. C Petrie, *King Charles III of Spain: An Enlightened Despot* (1971), p. 174. The Treaty of Utrecht was ratified by Queen Anne at Kensington

Palace on 31 July 1713. The contradiction in the phrases 'full and entire propriety' and 'without any territorial jurisdiction' is evident, and gave rise, repeatedly, to debate on whether ownership of the Rock was ever intended to pass from Madrid to London. Another matter entirely was whether the terms of the treaty had been observed. See note 15, below.

9. Plá, p. 46.
10. Bradford, pp. 57–8. See also Plá, p. 11.
11. Drinkwater, p. 20.
12. Cornwell, p. 13.
13. Bradford, pp. 60–1.
14. J Russell, *Gibraltar Besieged, 1779–1783* (1965), pp. 15–16.
15. The 1777 Census of the population in Gibraltar showed that 27% were Jewish, in plain contravention of the terms of the Treaty of Utrecht as it related to the Rock. See L Madway, 'Sefarad But Not Spain' (Yale University thesis, 1993).
16. Petrie, p. 178.
17. J Heriot, *An Historical Sketch of Gibraltar, with an Account of the Siege* (1792), p. 11.
18. Sir Robert Boyd, Lieutenant General (1710–1794). Deputy Governor of Gibraltar both before and during the siege, Boyd had served with distinction at Minden in 1759, and in the earlier siege of Minorca, as an official of the Board of Ordnance. He was subsequently appointed Colonel of the 39th Regiment of Foot, and proved to be a capable second-in-command on the Rock to Eliott, although he was in poor health. Boyd succeeded as Governor of Gibraltar on Eliott's death.
19. Russell, p. 36. Lord Weymouth was the sole Secretary of State at this time.
20. F Sayer, *The History of Gibraltar* (1865), p. 278.
21. S Ancell, *A Circumstantial Journal of the Long and Tedious Blockade and Siege of Gibraltar, 1779–1783* (1784), p. 58.
22. This additional training was required despite the newly raised regiment being reviewed on Datchet Common by George III, and 'going through their various manoeuvres with singular adroitness', according to a rather uncritical report in *The London Chronicle*, on 21 April 1778.
23. Drinkwater, p. 50.
24. Russell, p. 28.

Chapter 2: The Disagreeable Necessity

1. C Petrie, *King Charles III of Spain: An Enlightened Despot* (1971), p. 170.
2. Ibid., p. 181. The Spanish captains were unfamiliar with the tides, currents and shoals in the English Channel, and the French ships were short of provisions. The threat of invasion by combined fleet would prove to be more theoretical than real. See also D Macintyre, *Admiral Rodney* (1962), p. 95, and W James, *The British Navy in Adversity* (1926), p. 185. There was also some ill-feeling because the d'Orvilliers had command of the fleet, rather than Don Cordoba.
3. A Venning, *Following the Drum* (2005), p. 203.
4. J Drinkwater, *A History of the Late Siege of Gibraltar* (1785), p. 51.
5. B Cornwell, *A Description of Gibraltar, with an Account of the Blockade* (1782), pp. 22–3.
6. Petrie, p. 186.
7. S Ancell, *A Circumstantial Journal of the Long and Tedious Blockade and Siege of Gibraltar, 1779–1783* (1784), p. 8.
8. Drinkwater, p. 55.
9. The census showed that 9% of the civilian population was classed as 'Moroccan'. These may have been Spanish-born labourers from the enclave of Ceuta on the North African shore, and hence considered to be unreliable, unlike those born in Minorca, which was under British control.
10. Drinkwater, p. 56. The signal station on the highest point of the Rock had a clear view out across the Mediterranean, and could also see, and exchange signals with, ships approaching in the Atlantic Ocean far to the westward, before they rounded Cabrita Point. However, these same signals could also be seen by Spanish observers on the mainland, who would give warning of the approaching vessels before their own observers on the ground could do so. Once this breach of security was realized by the garrison, the signals were stopped.
11. Drinkwater, p. 59. Vice Admiral Antonio Don Barcelo (1717–97) was a tough and capable naval commander. Born into a humble Majorcan family, he had risen through the ranks, making for himself a fine reputation in the harsh operations to combat Barbary pirates operating along the Spanish coasts. His bold and skilful handling of

the light but powerfully armed lateen-rigged xebecs, the smaller nimble jabecquilla gunboats, galleys and other coastal craft, proved a constant source of concern to the garrison throughout the siege, and came as close as anything to bringing Eliott's efforts to grief. Don Barcelo undoubtedly failed to establish and maintain a close enough blockade of the Rock, and his error in allowing his squadron to go downwind when pursuing Captain Fagg in the privateer *Buck* left him out of position at a critical time. Still, he was a tough, knowing, and bruising commander and his eventual replacement was probably an error on the part of Madrid. See also J Harbron, *Trafalgar and the Spanish Navy: The Spanish Experience of Sea Power* (1988), p. xiv: 'Jabeque (*English* zebec or xebec) – A three-masted ship based on Arab naval architecture, each mast having a large lateen sail ... the Jabecque continued to be built as a warship up to 1826 and was well known in the eighteenth century Armada Espagnol ... often heavily armed and carrying between 32 and 40 guns.' The jabecquilla was the gunboat, the smaller cousin of the Jabeque/xebec.

12. Drinkwater, p. 60.
13. J Russell, *Gibraltar Besieged, 1779–1783* (1965), p. 44.
14. Drinkwater, pp. 62–3.
15. Ibid., p. 42.
16. Ancell, p. 6.
17. 'Britons Strike Home! Avenge Your Country's Cause! Protect Your King! Your Liberty! Your Laws!'
18. Venning, p. 205.
19. Ancell, pp. 7–8.
20. Drinkwater, p. 70. Lieutenant Henry Shrapnel, Royal Artillery, watched Mercier's experiment with air-burst shells with interest. He went on to develop the devastatingly effective anti-personnel projectile which still bears his name, although the term case-shot was also widely used.
21. Russell, p. 47.
22. Ancell, p. 14.
23. Ibid., pp. 8–9.
24. Russell, p. 118.
25. Drinkwater, p. 71.
26. Ancell, pp. 9–10.
27. Drinkwater, p. 78.

28. Ibid., p. 79.
29. Ancell, p. 18.
30. Ibid., pp. 19–20.
31. W James, pp. 187–8.
32. Ancell, pp. 21–2.
33. Cornwell, p. 27.
34. Russell, p. 51.
35. Drinkwater, p. 85.
36. Russell, p. 52.

Chapter 3: Moonlight Battles and Mountains of Fire

1. Sir George Brydges Rodney, Admiral (1718–92), entered the Royal Navy as a volunteer in 1732, becoming lieutenant seven years later. He was present at Hawke's victory off Ushant in 1747 in command of HMS *Eagle*, and was appointed Governor of Newfoundland in 1749. During the Seven Years' War, Rodney commanded HMS *Dublin*, and became Rear Admiral in 1759. He was commander-in-chief on the Leeward Islands station between 1761 and 1763, in which year he was made Vice Admiral of the Blue. After serving as a Member of Parliament, Rodney became Governor of Jamaica in 1771, and was made Rear Admiral soon afterwards. Deeply in debt, he then had to live in Paris to avoid his creditors, until a French benefactor paid off his liabilities, which enabled Rodney to take up command as commander-in-chief of the Leeward Islands station once more. His success against de Langara's Squadron in February 1780 was followed by the capture of the Dutch island of St Eustacius early in 1781, and the great naval victory over the French fleet, commanded by the Comte de Grasse, at the Battle of the Saintes on 12 April 1782. Created Baron Rodney in June 1782, the Admiral lived in retirement until his death in London on 24 May 1792.

2. Prince William (1765–1837), the third son of King George III of Great Britain, Ireland and Hanover, spent much of his early life in the Royal Navy, being present at the Moonlight Battle, visiting the besieged garrison in Gibraltar, and serving on the American seaboard during the War of Independence. In 1786, he was under Nelson in the West Indies, and had command of HMS *Andromeda* in 1788. The next year he became Rear Admiral, flying his flag in

HMS *Valiant*. William became Duke of Clarence in 1789, and finished his active sea-service the following year. In 1827 Clarence was appointed Lord High Admiral, although the post was relinquished the next year, and in 1830 he became King William IV on the death of his older brother, George IV. Affectionately known by many of his subjects as the 'Sailor King' for his courtly but rough and ready manners, he was also, less kindly, called 'Silly Billy' by his detractors, at a time of social ferment and political reform. William IV was childless, and when he died at Windsor Castle in 1837 he was succeeded by his young niece, Queen Victoria.

3. J Russell, *Gibraltar Besieged, 1779–1783* (1965), pp. 47–51. John Spilsbury acidly commented that 'The Governor does not care how dear things are.'

4. S Ancell, *A Circumstantial Journal of the Long and Tedious Blockade and Siege of Gibraltar, 1779–1783* (1784), p. 27.

5. Russell, p. 58. Vice Admiral Don Juan Francisco de Langara y Huarte (1736–1806), was present at the capture of Minorca from the British in 1759. From 1766 until 1771 he carried out a number of scientific expeditions when charting the Pacific coast of North America, and gained a reputation as a skilful navigator. He had to meet Rodney with a much reduced squadron on the afternoon of 16 January 1780, and fought a hopeless battle with great bravery. In 1793 de Langara was made Captain General of the Armada Espagnol, and took part in the capture of Toulon with a Royal Navy squadron under Admiral Sir Samuel Hood. De Langara distinguished himself by his very capable rearguard action during the Allied withdrawal from the arsenal. With the conclusion of a French and Spanish alliance, he was soon campaigning in support of Bonaparte in his Italian campaign, and in 1796 became Secretary of State for the Armada Espagnol, and Inspector General the following year. The Admiral retired from active service three years later.

6. O Warner, *Fighting Sail* (1979), p. 103. Coppering was initially used by the Royal Navy in 1761 to protect wooden hulls from the teredo worm in tropical waters. Rodney admired the design and construction of the Spanish warships, but not their foul un-coppered hulls. The Spanish naval commanders, paradoxically, benefited by the expertise of British shipbuilders who were often employed in

their shipyards. See also, J Harbron, *Trafalgar and the Spanish Navy: The Spanish Experience of Sea Power*, 1988.

7. P Trew, *Rodney and the Breaking of the Line* (2006), p. 54.
8. P Hore, *The Habit of Victory* (2005), p. 115.
9. Ibid.
10. G Mundy, *The Life and Correspondence of the late Admiral Lord Rodney* (1830), vol. 1, p. 222.
11. T McGuffie, *The Siege of Gibraltar, 1779–1783* (1964), p. 57.
12. Mundy, vol. 1, p. 223.
13. J Plá, *Gibraltar* (1955), p. 82.
14. W Kingston, *How Britannia Came to Rule the Waves* (1900).
15. Mundy, vol. 1, pp. 220–1. The Spanish squadron destroyed or captured by Rodney in the Moonlight Battle comprised – *Fenix* (80), *Diligente* (70), *Monarca* (70), *Princessa* (70), *San Domingo* (70, blown up), *San Eugenio* (70 – beached and abandoned), while the following ships managed to escape: *San Julian* (70 – taken and re-captured), *San Lorenzo* (70), *San Augustin* (70), *San Rosalie* (26) and *San Cecilia* (28). Two others, *San Genaro* (74) and *San Justo* (74) had lost contact with de Langara before the action began, and also escaped.
16. J Drinkwater, *A History of the Late Siege of Gibraltar* (1785), pp. 90–1.
17. Drinkwater, p. 95. Prince William discharged his duty as a relatively humble Midshipman, but it would be absurd to imagine that the King's son did not receive some occasional special treatment.
18. Mundy, vol. 1, pp. 238–9. See also F Sayer, *The History of Gibraltar* (1865), pp. 311–12.
19. Russell, p. 63.
20. Sayer, p. 305.
21. Russell, p. 61.
22. Drinkwater, p. 103.
23. B Cornwell, *A Description of Gibraltar, with an Account of the Blockade* (1782), p. 24. See also E Bradford, *Gibraltar: The History of a Fortress* (1971), pp. 89–90, for comments on the state of Eliott's supplies, and the ration scales in use at this time.
24. Russell, p. 74.
25. Bradford, p. 92.
26. Cornwell, p. 18.
27. Drinkwater, pp. 111–12.
28. Cornwell, p. 19.

29. Ancell, p. 49.
30. Cornwell, p. 17.
31. Russell, p. 81.
32. A Venning, *Following the Drum* (2005), pp. 207–8.
33. Ross's regimental rank was Lieutenant Colonel, but his rank in the army was Colonel. Robert Boyd, a Lieutenant General, was Colonel of the 39th Foot, a throwback to the time when senior officers raised and 'owned' their regiment, before becoming a largely honorary title.
34. Russell, p. 83. See McGuffie, pp. 79–80, for interesting comments on Ross's conduct in this strange affair of the address to the 39th Foot.

Chapter 4: These Infernal Spit-fires

1. Some reports say a lump sum of £7.5 million was paid over by Madrid to the Sultan, but this seems unlikely, as such a massive amount, once paid, was certainly gone whether or not the agreement held.
2. S Ancell, *A Circumstantial Journal of the Long and Tedious Blockade and Siege of Gibraltar, 1779–1783* (1784), p. 57.
3. J Drinkwater, *A History of the Late Siege of Gibraltar* (1785), pp. 185–6.
4. Ancell, p. 66.
5. Drinkwater, pp. 120–1.
6. Ancell, p. 71.
7. B Cornwell, *A Description of Gibraltar, with an Account of the Blockade* (1782), p. 10.
8. Ancell, p. 85.
9. Drinkwater, pp. 138–9.
10. Ancell, p. 102.
11. Drinkwater, p. 141.
12. Russell, p. 100.
13. A Venning, *Following the Drum* (2005), p. 206.
14. J Russell, *Gibraltar Besieged, 1779–1783* (1965), p. 122.
15. F Sayer, *The History of Gibraltar* (1865), pp. 363–4.
16. Venning, p. 208.
17. C Petrie, *King Charles III of Spain: An Enlightened Despot* (1971), p. 195.
18. Drinkwater, p. 147.
19. Cornwell, p. 29.
20. Ibid., p. 31.

21. Ancell, pp. 111–15.
22. Drinkwater, p. 152.
23. Russell, p. 125. See also Venning, p. 207.
24. Ancell, p. 107.
25. Ibid., pp. 121–2.
26. Ibid., p. 107.
27. Russell, p. 118.
28. Ancell, p. 109.
29. Drinkwater, p. 157.
30. Ancell, p. 131. See also Russell, p. 121, for a slightly different account.
31. T McGuffie, *The Siege of Gibraltar, 1779–1783* (1964), p. 96.
32. Drinkwater, p. 163.
33. Russell, p. 123.
34. Ancell, p. 132.
35. Petrie, p. 193.

Chapter 5: This Glorious Occasion

1. S Ancell, *A Circumstantial Journal of the Long and Tedious Blockade and Siege of Gibraltar, 1779–1783* (1784), p. 118.
2. A Venning, *Following the Drum* (2005), p. 211.
3. Ibid., p. 122.
4. J Drinkwater, *A History of the Late Siege of Gibraltar* (1785), pp. 192–3.
5. Ancell, pp. 103–4.
6. Ibid., pp. 143–67.
7. Drinkwater, p. 189.
8. E Bradford, *Gibraltar: The History of a Fortress* (1971), p. 108.
9. Russell, pp. 147–8.
10. J Heriot, *An Historical Sketch of Gibraltar, with an Account of the Siege* (1792), p. 72.
11. Russell, p. 153.
12. Ibid., p. 151.
13. Ibid. It is more than likely that Ross suspected Eliott of trying to pilfer some of the credit for the operation, when the garrison commander had no role or place being so far forward that night.
14. Heriot, p. 83.
15. Bradford, p. 113.

16. F Sayer, *The History of Gibraltar* (1865), p. 363.
17. Heriot, p. 72.
18. Ancell, p. 177.
19. Bradford, p. 112.
20. Ancell, p. 178.
21. Russell, p. 153.
22. Drinkwater, p. 210.
23. Ancell, pp. 183–4.
24. C Petrie, *King Charles III of Spain: An Enlightened Despot* (1971), p. 119.
25. Ancell, p. 197.
26. Drinkwater, pp. 234–5.
27. Henry Ince was granted a commission for his efforts in the siege tunnels. On his retirement he was presented with a plot of land on the upper slopes of the Rock, known thereafter as Ince's Farm.
28. J Plá, *Gibraltar* (1955), p. 57.
29. Ancell, p. 215.

Chapter 6: An Equal Share of Glory

1. S Ancell, *A Circumstantial Journal of the Long and Tedious Blockade and Siege of Gibraltar, 1779–1783* (1784), pp. 219–20.
2. Ancell, pp. 231–2.
3. J Drinkwater, *A History of the Late Siege of Gibraltar* (1785), p. 255. Some accounts say Caleb Huntly rather than Hartley.
4. Louis de Balba de Berton, Comte (Duc) de Crillon (1717–96) took over the command of the Spanish and French forces blockading Gibraltar in 1782, after successfully capturing Minorca from the British. The son of a noble family, he entered the Royal Guard as a cadet at the age of fourteen, and was then commissioned into the Bretagne Régiment, rising to become Colonel in 1738. De Crillon was wounded at the battle of Rossbach in 1757, and distinguished himself while on campaign in Spain and Portugal while in the service of Madrid. He was made Duc de Mahon after the capture of Minorca in February 1782, and became a Spanish Grandee. Although he was well aware of the substantial nature of the Gibraltar defences, and exasperated at the seemingly lax way the siege and blockade had been handled before his appointment, de Crillon

nonetheless undertook the task with great energy, and his failure had little impact upon his reputation.

5. Drinkwater, pp. 268–9. See also, C Petrie, *King Charles III of Spain: An Enlightened Despot* (1971), p. 200, and J Plá, *Gibraltar* (1955), pp. 85–6 for a different version.

6. F Sayer, *The History of Gibraltar* (1865), pp. 373–5.

7. Plá, p. 88.

8. J Russell, *Gibraltar Besieged, 1779–1783* (1965), p. 189.

9. Ibid., pp. 191–2.

10. Petrie, p. 201.

11. Drinkwater, p. 293.

12. Ancell, pp. 255–6.

13. Russell, p. 180.

14. T McGuffie, *The Siege of Gibraltar, 1779–1783* (1964), p. 156. An observer noted scornfully that the Spanish gun-crews were so ill-trained and managed that they continued firing, at nothing, even after the ships had completed their run and turned away into Gibraltar Bay.

15. Drinkwater, p. 288.

16. Ancell, pp. 258–9.

17. Plá, p. 88.

18. Ancell, p. 262.

19. Drinkwater, p. 298.

20. Anon., *The Gloucester Journal*, 14 October 1782.

21. H Howes, *Gibraltar and its Sieges* (1884), p. 95.

22. Drinkwater, pp. 296–7.

23. Plá, p. 88.

24. Howes, p. 95.

25. Drinkwater, p. 297.

26. Plá, p. 88.

27. Sayer, pp. 393–4.

28. Howes, p. 95.

29. Russell, p. 247.

30. Extract from a poem on the Battle of Lepanto in 1571.

31. McGuffie, p. 163.

32. Ancell, pp. 262–5.

33. Petrie, pp. 202–3.

34. Russell, pp. 255–6.

35. J Barrow, *The Life of Richard, Earl Howe, K.G.* (1838), p. 149.
36. Ibid., p. 150.
37. Drinkwater, p. 332. Admiral Sir Richard Howe (1726–99), affectionately known to the seamen as 'Black Dick', entered the Royal Navy at age fourteen. He accompanied Anson on his voyage to the South Seas, and fought under Hawke at Quiberon Bay in 1759, having become a Viscount the previous year. Howe accomplished the third relief of Gibraltar late in 1782, in the face of a significantly more powerful Spanish and French naval force. He did, however, refuse to fully engage his opponents off Cape Spartel on the return voyage, and this course of action attracted criticism. In command of the Channel Fleet at the outbreak of the Revolutionary Wars, Howe achieved a great naval victory over the French at the 'Glorious 1st of June' in 1794 although, arguably, his most notable success was the relief of Gibraltar late in 1782.
38. Barrow, p. 153.
39. Drinkwater, p. 344.
40. Barrow, p. 157.
41. Russell, pp. 292–3.
42. E Bradford, *Gibraltar: The History of a Fortress* (1971), p. 131.
43. Russell, pp. 271–2.
44. Drinkwater, p. 351.

Chapter 7: That Proud Fortress

1. M Harvey, *Gibraltar: A History* (1996), p. 102.
2. C Petrie, *King Charles III of Spain: An Enlightened Despot* (1971), p. 214. It is likely the French had no great wish to see Great Britain and Spain in amicable agreement, with the Rock being given up by London. A lasting enmity between the two countries would limit the freedom of action of both, to the benefit of France.
3. J Plá, *Gibraltar* (1955), p. 95.
4. Harvey, p. 104.
5. J Russell, *Gibraltar Besieged, 1779–1783* (1965), p. 259. Minorca was recaptured by the British in 1798, but given up in 1802, as the valuable and more defensible port at Valletta in Malta was then in use by the Royal Navy.
6. E Bradford, *Gibraltar: The History of a Fortress* (1971), p. 133. The

regular truce-boat was just one of many instances of courteous and gallant conduct between the opposing sides.

7. J Harbron, *Trafalgar and the Spanish Navy: The Spanish Experience of Sea Power* (1988), p. 144.
8. Russell, p. 281.
9. J Drinkwater, *A History of the Late Siege of Gibraltar* (1785), p. 354.
10. Bradford, p. 134.
11. Drinkwater, p. 361.
12. T McGuffie, *The Siege of Gibraltar, 1779–1783* (1964), p. 191.
13. J Plá, pp. 74–5.
14. Ibid., pp. 78–9. King Charles III's loyalty to his field commanders, and his reluctance to replace them even when their efforts were plainly faltering, was admirable, but contributed to their overall lack of performance. Secure in their positions and privileges, they rarely ventured far enough to be put to the test.
15. Russell, p. 33.

Appendix 3

1. 'With Eliott to Glory and Victory.' T McGuffie, *The Siege of Gibraltar, 1779–1783* (1964), p. 193.
2. E Bradford, *Gibraltar: The History of a Fortress* (1971), p. 75. See also, E Junger, *Storm of Steel* (1920, 1961), trans. M Hoffmann, p. 19. Ernst Junger served in the 73rd Prinz Albrecht's during World War I.

Bibliography

Three contemporary accounts of the Great Siege, written by British soldiers who took an active part in the operations – John Drinkwater of the 72nd Regiment of Foot, John Spilsbury of the 12th Foot, and Samuel Ancell of the 58th Foot – provide considerable (and sometimes rather repetitious) details on the day-to-day life in Gibraltar during this time. Drinkwater's memoirs, the draft of which was almost destroyed by a Spanish shell on Christmas Day 1782, were published in Liverpool in 1784, shortly after the 72nd Foot was disbanded. This proved very popular, and was reprinted several times. John Drinkwater was said to be the last living survivor of the Great Siege, dying in Surrey in 1844, aged eighty-one. Spilsbury's account of the siege was edited and published in Gibraltar in 1908, but Ancell's 'Journal', on the other hand, was drawn from extracts of the detailed letters that he regularly wrote to his brother in England. The instant, very fresh, nature of Ancell's description of daily events lends particular clarity, together with a certain dry wit, to his account: 'Last night came in a schooner from Malaga with lemons and oranges. They are natives of Spain, but run in here, knowing it to be a good market.' He did, however, feel it necessary to change the title of his journal in later editions, omitting the word 'tedious' to give it more immediate appeal with the reading public. The lively journals of Mrs Katherine Upton and Mrs Miriam Green, both 'on the strength' as army wives with their children in the garrison, also make interesting, and occasionally quite harrowing, reading. Unfortunately, Miriam Green's health was broken by the effects of the siege and she died soon after returning to England in 1783. The individual writers, spectators and participants in the siege drew in the main upon memory, and there is the occasional discrepancy over dates and precise details of the same incident.

Ancell, S, *A Circumstantial Journal of the Long and Tedious Blockade and Siege of Gibraltar, 1779–1783* (1784).
Anon., *Mémoires pour servir à l'histoire du siège de Gibraltar* (1783) (Royal Engineers Library).

——, *The London Chronicle*, 21 April 1778.

——, *The Gloucester Journal*, October and November 1782.

Atkinson, C T, *The Dorsetshire Regiment*, vol. 1 (1947).

Bamfield, V, *On the Strength: The Story of the British Army Wife* (1974).

Barrow, J, *The Life of Richard, Earl Howe, K.G.* (1838).

Beatson, R, *Naval and Military Memoirs of Great Britain, 1727–1783*, vol. 5 (1804).

Bradford, E, *Gibraltar: The History of a Fortress* (1971).

Cannon, R, *Historical Record of the 39th Regiment of Foot* (1853).

——, *Historical Record of the 56th Regiment of Foot* (1844).

Chartrand, R, *The Great Siege of Gibraltar, 1779–1783* (2006).

Chevalier, E, *Histoire de la Marine Française* (1877).

Conn, S, *Gibraltar in British Diplomacy in the 18th Century* (1942).

Cornwell, B, *A Description of Gibraltar, with an Account of the Blockade* (1782).

Dalton, J, *The Rock and the Royal Artillery* (RA Journal) (1924).

Drinkwater, J, *A History of the Late Siege of Gibraltar* (1785; also 1905 edition).

Fa, D, and Finlayson, C, *The Fortifications of Gibraltar, 1068–1945* (2006).

Falkner, J, 'George Augustus Eliott, 1st Baron Heathfield of Gibraltar' (*Dictionary of National Biography*, 2004).

——, *Marlborough's Wars: Eye-Witness Accounts* (2005).

Fortescue, J, *History of the British Army*, vol. 3 (1911).

Grant, J, *British Battles on Land and Sea*, (1880).

Harbron, J, *Trafalgar and the Spanish Navy: The Spanish Experience of Sea Power* (1988).

Harvey, M, *Gibraltar: A History* (1996).

Heriot, J, *An Historical Sketch of Gibraltar, with an Account of the Siege* (1792).

Holloway, C, *Journal of the Blockade and Siege of Gibraltar* (Royal Engineers Library Mss).

Hore, P, *The Habit of Victory* (2005).

Howes, H, *Gibraltar and its Sieges* (1884).

James, J, *The History of the Herculean Straits* (1771).

James, W, *The British Navy in Adversity* (1926).

Junger, E, *Storm of Steel*, trans. M Hoffman (1920 and 1961).

Kenyon, R (ed.), *A Lady's Experiences in the Great Siege of Gibraltar* (Mrs M Green's Diary, Royal Engineers Journal, 1912).

Kingston, W, *How Britannia Came to Rule the Waves* (1900).

Ledesma, M, *Gibraltar, la Roca de Calpe* (1957).

Macintyre, D, *Admiral Rodney* (1962).

Mackesey, P, *The War for America, 1775–1783* (1964).

Madway, L, 'Sefarad but not Spain' (Yale University thesis, 1993).

McGuffie, T, *The Siege of Gibraltar, 1779–1783* (1964).

Montferrier, S, *Le siège de Gibraltar en 1782* (1810).

Muller, J, *The Attac and Defence of Fortified Places* [sic] (1757).

Mundy, G, *The Life and Correspondence of the late Admiral Lord Rodney* (1830).

Oatts, L, *Proud Heritage: The Story of the Highland Light Infantry* (1952).

Palao, G, *The Guns and Towers of Gibraltar* (1975).

Petrie, C, *King Charles III of Spain: An Enlightened Despot* (1971).

Plá, J, *Gibraltar* (1955).

Porter, R, *History of the Corps of Royal Engineers*, vol. 1 (1889).

Rodger, N, *The Command of the Ocean* (2005).

Russell, J, *Gibraltar Besieged, 1779–1783* (1965).

Saarinen, A, *The Moonlight Battle, 16 January 1780* (2003).

Sanchez, M, *Writing the Rock of Gibraltar, 1720–1890* (2006).

Sayer, F, *The History of Gibraltar* (1865).

Spilsbury, J, *A Journal of the Siege of Gibraltar, 1779–1783*, ed. H Frere (1908).

Spinney, D, *Rodney* (1969).

Trew, P, *Rodney and the Breaking of the Line* (2006).

Venning, A, *Following the Drum* (2005).

Warner, O, *Fighting Sail* (1979).

Index